T

Teach Happy
Educating Wellness for Teacher and Student Success

Lisa Canova

Copyright © Lisa Canova 2017.

Published by Teach Happy, LLC.
2299 4th Street, Boulder, CO. 80302

All rights reserved. No part of this book may be reproduced in whole or in part without written permission from the publisher.

ISBN: 9780998905808 for print book
ISBN: 9780998905815 for ebook

Cover design by Madeeha Shaikh (DezignManiac, Freelance designer @99designs.com)
dezignmaniac99@gmail.com.

In memory of Professor Shelby Wolf

Contents

Introduction

Section I. Begin Making the Connection

1. Human Connection: "Every Kid Needs a Champion" (17)
2. Subbing Is How to Start (28)
3. The Power of Playground Observation (36)

Section II. Finding Teacher Wellness

4. Why Teacher Wellness? (48)
5. Maintaining Wellness: "Control Versus No Control" Within the Public Education System (62)
6. Being Empowered (67)

Section III. Creating an Effective Teaching Environment

7. Teacher Effectiveness: Making Learning Useful and Entertaining (72)
8. Time's a-Wastin': Standardized Testing (76)
9. Mindful Classroom Management (86)
10. Social and Emotional Wellness of Students (94)

Section IV. Teaching that Promotes Student Wellness

11. Wellness Without the Labels (106)
12. Supporting Student Behavior: Rethinking ADHD (113)
13. Fostering Student Self-Esteem: An Anecdote to Bullying (122)
14. Tolerance and Acceptance = Empathy (131)
15. Health Wellness: Preventing the Cycle of Abuse (136)

Section V. Necessary Practice: Social-Emotional Learning

16. Learning "Dangerous Truths" Through Literature (150)
17. Service Learning Breeds Spirit (160)
18. Indigenous Education (165)
19. Finland Has It Figured Out! (180)

Conclusion (184)

Acknowledgments (187)

"UNLESS someone like you cares a whole awful lot, nothing is going to get better. It's not."

—Theodor Seuss Geisel (Dr. Seuss), *The Lorax*

Introduction

The quality of a teacher's health and wellness determines how joyful, curious, creative, and productive their classroom has the potential to become. Intuitively, it makes sense that a teacher's state affects their classroom climate—either positively or negatively— yet, realistically, it is often difficult to feel the power of this influence.

Teaching presents challenges, and every once in a while we hit a wall, smack dab in the face. Sometimes hurting more, sometimes less. But the more we feel supported and work at taking care of ourselves, the better prepared we are to handle and face head-on the bumps in the road as they arise.

Having taught in the public school system and worked in special education and talented and gifted programs, I witnessed firsthand how a teacher's sense of self impacts the well-being of students. I have been fortunate to observe many excellent teachers, and while receiving my master's degree in literacy, had the pleasure of working with one of the most amazing and inspiring professors I have ever met.

My goal in writing this book is to give both new and veteran teachers the wellness coaching and support they deserve. Teaching is a unique job that is wonderful when the person doing the job feels wonderful as well. How fortunate teachers are to have the power and the resources to do a lot of good in this world! Teaching is hard, no doubt, but the reward is much greater than any professional hardship. I want teachers not to feel limited by self-imposed constraints and stress, which only increases the likelihood of burnout and leaving the career. That is why this book provides real stories, tools, and suggestions for innovative approaches and hopefully moments of *I never thought of that before . . .*

Human Connection in Education

Teach Happy: Educating Wellness for Teacher and Student Success focuses on the value of human connection and the importance this has in being an effective educator. Human connection is also at the root of the social and emotional wellness we want for our students. In a 2014 *New York Times* op-ed titled "Teaching Is Not a Business," David L. Kirp states: "While technology can be put to good use by talented teachers, they, and not the futurists, must take the lead. The process of teaching and learning is an intimate act that neither computers nor markets can hope to replicate. Small wonder, then, that the business model hasn't worked in reforming the schools—there is simply no substitute for the personal element."

The most important part of teaching wellness for educators and students is a deep understanding of human connection. I define this as a relationship between student and teacher based upon trust, mutual respect, kindness, courtesy, feeling safe, the ability to take risks, and even failing at times. Teachers have the wonderful gift and power of creating the most exceptional experience for themselves and their students. This power also includes avoiding circumstances that drain and deplete their vital energy and the intention to make a difference. My desire is to support teachers by helping develop ways to feel confidence, inner wellness, and fulfillment in the job, and maintain this wellness over time.

Establishing a human connection with parents is important as well. Reaching out via phone, or setting up a quick face-to-face meeting to express positive feedback about a student or a concern, always strengthens connection further than an e-mail. It also shows you care, and parents can feel this and feel heard. It is all about feeling heard. I resolved more potential conflicts and misunderstandings as an educator once I figured this out. Receiving parental support strengthens the trust you are building with your students.

Once you have established a human connection with your students, it can then spread beyond the classroom into the greater community and globally. Many good teachers already know and practice this. Other teachers are stuck and find it difficult to create or maintain this connection and passion for continued work in an educational system geared toward not always putting students first. Then there are ambitious individuals, energetic and idealistic, studying to become educators, and it is important for them—before entering the profession—to understand the premise of being happy and establishing human connection with students early on.

It sounds so simple, the whole human connection thing, but it isn't. When I started teaching elementary students, the world was shifting into technology overload. There are now many ways to disconnect from personal relationships—the Internet, phones, and other distractions—that can prevent human connection. This leaves feelings of being lost and needing to belong. A typical public school classroom contains a large, diverse group of students who arrive every day with an inability to feel empathy, get along with others, and lack tools to manage personal feelings. Not to mention insufficient academic and cognitive skills.

So, then, how does one find the balance and their personal recipe for being well and teaching wellness success? It is through teachers adapting social and emotional instruction for students that improves academic learning and success for students—basic social skills and conversational habits essential to personal well-being and evolution. Part of the recipe for human connection with students is just loving to teach.

Throughout my professional career in different educational roles, one thing was constant: I loved teaching children and learned so much from their amazing minds. But truth be told, there were years during which I was not happy in the role for other reasons. Yet it was my own doing and responsibility for this unhappiness. During those times, I was not administering the self-care needed to ease the stress and disappointment I felt sometimes from my administration, other colleagues, and the bureaucracy of the public school system. I found it hard to stay focused on why I entered the job in the first place—to learn and make a positive impact—and lacked appropriate boundaries to keep my energy high and curiosity peeked. I lacked sleep and stopped exercising in the way needed for me to keep my physical body feeling good. I spent many a night drowning worries associated with student progress with red wine and was consistently getting sick and acquiring new and different cold/flu viruses. I had to learn that conserving energy for my job enabled me to do better. I also had to learn what tools and routines I needed for personal wellness, how to develop healthy relationships with colleagues, and how to create the right professional environment of support. For me, the teaching part came naturally. It was the reality of extraneous job requirements and dealing with the bureaucracy and school environment that did not come so naturally. Eventually, I learned that managing and understanding ways to work within the system and find positive outlets and supports to maintain health, energy, creativity, and inspiration was the best way to go.

   Western teaching models may feel all business sometimes, with standardized testing and technology-informed academic standards, but it is really about engaged students, challenging and useful curriculum, and the individual teacher leading the charge. Teaching requires individuals to take on big responsibilities, brave approaches, and extensive risks. Although I was one individual in a sea of open-ended challenges, large class sizes, socioeconomic constraints, and administrative mandates, I learned to take solace and empowerment in knowing that once I closed my classroom door, it was up to me to find a way to make magic with students. I later realized I had ultimate control over my classroom and was never limited to the possibility for daily positive impacts.

    Jonathan Kozol, the great American writer, educator, and activist, best known for his efforts to improve public education, states, "Pick battles big enough to matter, small enough to win." The social and emotional health and wellness of our teachers and students is our battle. This book calls for educational grassroots change in focusing on wellness education first. Starting with just one teacher and spreading is how students will win.

Section I
Begin Making the Connection

"Great teachers empathize with kids, respect them, and believe that each one has something special that can be built upon."

—Ann Lieberman, EdD
Professor Emeritus of Education at Teachers College, Columbia University.

1
Human Connection: "Every Kid Needs a Champion"

Rita Pierson is an example of an educator who championed human connection among children. She passed away in June of 2013, at age sixty-one, but during her forty years in education, Rita worked as an elementary, junior high, and special education teacher; administrator; counselor; and testing coordinator. She eventually conducted workshops for teachers on techniques for teaching and supporting underserved populations. Throughout her career, Rita believed that teachers should strive to get to know their students and show them how much they matter—and support them in their growth, no matter how modest.

    I learned about Rita Pierson through a powerful TED Talk she gave in May, 2013, titled "Every Kid Needs a Champion." Her talk was simple but profound, and I felt very moved by her message of *the importance of connection*. Connection and human relationships. Rita mentions how educational-reform advocates cite numerous reasons why kids don't learn—the biggies being poverty, low attendance, and negative influences from family and peers. While these factors clearly play a role in learning, I have also found that not only do kids not learn from people they do not like, but students need to like, respect, and feel challenged, safe, and nurtured by the educators who teach them. *They learn better from those teachers who create a classroom community where students feel cared for and loved.* Rita was one of those teachers.

In her talk, Rita tells a story of how one colleague said to her, "They do not pay me to like the kids. They pay me to teach a lesson and kids should learn it." I too have had experiences with teachers who convey the mindset "I am not here to be their friend" or "I am their senior and authority—students are to obey the rules and do as they are told." My favorite story from Rita's talk is when she recounts teaching a lesson on ratios and afterward checks her guide from the teacher's edition, realizing she has taught the whole lesson wrong. The next day she apologizes to her students and tells them of her mistake. Her students reveal that some knew she was off the mark but did not want to interrupt her enthusiasm and momentum. They kindly accepted her apology and expressed appreciation for her passion for trying, even though her approach was incorrect.

She also recounts teaching students who are extremely academically deficient, and describes her fear and struggles with facing the difficulty in raising self-esteem and academic achievement at the same time. When a student of Rita's missed eighteen out of twenty questions on an exam, Rita put "+2" on the paper plus a smiley face. The student asked her if he had gotten an F and she said yes.

"Why did you put the smiley face, then?"

"Because you are on a roll. You got two right. You did not miss all of them. We will review this and you will do better next time, won't you?"

"Yes, ma'am, I can do better!!"

Rita realized how "−18" sucks the energy and power out of kids to do better, whereas "+2" says that something is better than nothing and the student's attempt was not all bad. Rita also mentions that it is not realistic for teachers to like all their students. You never hear this in education classes at the university level. But let's be real here. Just as you may not like every person or colleague you come into contact with throughout your lifetime, it is not reasonable or possible to like every student you have. I agree with Rita that our toughest students never miss a day of school, even when we need a break, and they show up for us for a reason. I really do believe that. It all comes back to human connection and relationships.

There will always be a policy we do not agree with or does not make sense, the administrator or superintendent who does not serve the best interests of students, the lack of financial incentive, but there will always be the opportunity to override these things with empowering students through our relationship with them. As Rita so beautifully says, "Teaching and learning should bring joy."

Building Human Connection Between Student and Teacher

How powerful would our world be if we had kids who were not afraid to think, take risks, and who had a champion? Every child deserves this—an adult who never gives up on them, understands the power of connection, insists that they become the best person they can possibly be, and respects who they are as individuals.

How powerful would it be if our world had *teachers* who were not afraid to think, take risks, understand the power of connection, and feel courageous enough to be that champion? So many things today take us away from the personal and connection: technology, overbooking ourselves with activities and projects, overmedicating children and adults, too much testing. Way too much testing. So much of teaching is the connection between student and educator.

You will certainly have students who will test that connection. But those students are there for a reason, as Rita reminds us. They are some of our own greatest teachers, and they hold big surprises too. In fact, it is seeing the success in working with such students that can make all the difference in shifting our teaching to be more meaningful, one student at a time.

Teachers have the power to change the proverbial "most likely to succeed" into "more likely to succeed." With the support of parents, teachers can collectively force the educational system to pivot and turn itself up on its side. It won't be easy, but big changes often are not. What follows are some important ways that new and veteran teachers alike can build human connection with their students.

Establish Respect Between Student and Teacher

Respect is earned—not given or demanded—and the process of establishing respect between student and teacher is a two-way street. It is especially important for new teachers to recognize this.

      Teachers are role models. Instead of complaining that kids talk back, act out, and misbehave, be the person you want your students to be. Be a person of character and integrity. When students first meet you at the beginning of the year, they are sizing you up and preparing how to respond. Your presence will determine their response. Think about how you approach students, speak, and respond. Are you confident? Be aware of your choice of words. Do you take pride in your appearance and dress? As someone who loves wearing sweatpants and casual wear, I know this approach does not bode well in professional and classroom settings. As for the stereotypical holiday sweater worn by many teachers, yuck! Unless you have a very good sense of humor and are following an ugly sweater trend resurgence, just say no. Time to upgrade and be current. Students will want to rise to the occasion, and if they conclude that you respect yourself, they too will respect you and want to emulate the desirable human qualities you are modeling.

Practice What You Preach (Because Kids Have a Strong B.S. Detector)

If you are not straightforward and honest about something (like Rita not knowing how to teach ratios but acknowledging her mistake and apologizing the next day), kids always know. Students may wonder, *does my teacher really mean what she/he says?* And they may ask you, "Is what we're learning now going to matter down the road?" They are intuitive and insightful beings, and they know if you are not true to your word. Your answers to their questions should be well thought out because they are critical to building credibility in the classroom. *Is* what you are teaching going to be potentially useful in their lives? If so, give examples of how. Be prepared for this type of questioning, and have some answers in mind. If the material is not relevant or useful, why are you teaching it? If you do not know the answer to something, let students know you do not know but would like to learn. Or choose not to teach the material and explain why, substituting what will be useful for your students. Also, remember to model behavior that takes the high road by doing what is ethically right, even if it's not easy or popular.

Students are always watching, listening, and observing their teachers. Sound familiar, parents? When it comes to creating connection with students, not only are you practicing what you preach, but what you teach!

LISTEN, Pause, OBSERVE, Pause

Listen closely to what kids are saying, as well as what they are not saying. A student's nonverbal behavior offers clues about what is going on for them personally as well as their level of understanding of what is being taught. Eye contact, body language conveying that you are engaged, and showing enthusiasm for what is being said indicate good listening skills. They also model excellent social skills for students. Pause before reacting to a situation that may signal a potential problem. Always pause and think.

Think through what the student's behavior is telling you. Everything in the teaching day tends to be rushed. We rush from subject to subject, project to project, and it is important to slow things down. With every student behavior, there is a reason behind the behavior, whether positive or negative or somewhere in between. Taking time to think this through could result in a better solution to help the student succeed in their learning environment.

Create a Safe Zone in the Classroom

Kids know through the visuals on walls and the encouraging, inclusive words spoken frequently by teachers that their classroom (and school) is a place of acceptance and tolerance of individual differences. Student diversity is encouraged and welcomed. Always. Derogatory language and disrespectful behavior is not tolerated. Never.

At the beginning of the year, have students create pithy posters to decorate the classroom environment—and even volunteer to decorate the hallways. Also, students and teacher can generate a classroom "agreements" poster, map, or giant quilt (yes, this was done by a fabulous teacher friend and parent who made it that much more special) that they can strive to live by while at school. Each student and teacher can then initial or sign their name to the agreements. All students and adults are to be encouraged and accepted for their individual differences and identity, including and not limited to sexual orientation, race, gender, creed, or religion.

The goal, then, is that throughout the year, teachers—with the help of parent volunteers or students—hang artwork and other examples of student work, chosen by students, to display proudly throughout the classroom. One of my favorite fourth- and fifth-grade pithy posters said, "Be powerful—not powerless." It was simple and often used as a platform for discussion around many school-related issues, both academic and social. It was great to hear what those words meant to students and watch them work through these issues in the classroom.

*　*　*

Each year, new student groups will bring a different dynamic and different energy to your classroom, but one thing is constant: You can depend on your ability to build human connection with each new group given to you. Human connection is a key ingredient to the success of the teacher-student relationship. Some students will present more challenges than others, but this adds stimulation to the job and an opportunity for you to develop new strategies and skills. In the following pages, you will find a number of perspectives and approaches to help you feel more confident and effective in navigating the challenges the profession provides.

2
Subbing Is How to Start

"I hear and I forget. I see and I remember. I do and I understand." This popular quote, attributed to the Chinese philosopher Confucius, can be applied to teaching. Before I taught children, I would hear both what and what not to do. I watched veteran teachers—some good, some better—and considered how their experiences and approaches could apply to my own classroom. Once I began teaching, I started to understand.

Whether you are a new or veteran educator, there are always new approaches and suggestions to bettering and enhancing your teaching practice. Most new teachers who enter the public school system are hopeful and determined to make a difference. That is why they enter the profession. At the start, we tend to be idealistic, enthusiastic to work with children, and believe we will be preparing our students with skills that will be useful for life. While I was studying to become a teacher, I was (and still am) determined to change the lives of children for the better.

I began substitute teaching to supplement my income and learned firsthand what I was getting myself into, so to speak. It is when I began working as a sub in different public schools that I started to truly understand what it meant to teach. Some days I laughed, some days I cried, and others I managed to hang on by a thread until I heard the bell signaling that school was out. After about six months of free-agent subbing, I landed a short-term sub gig at an inner city school located in Denver, Colorado.

Substitute teaching is challenging, but it is an excellent way to determine whether you are really up to pursuing an education job in the first place. It solidifies the necessity for establishing human connection with students right away. Even when you do that, the job as a sub is still fresh with challenges that mimic real teaching.

It was through my early subbing experiences that I became aware of how taking care of myself was crucial to taking care of others and creating a healthy and productive work and learning environment. My short-term job at the inner city school was as a second-grade teacher. The school sat literally right next to a professional football stadium and was often shadowed by the ominous structure. At the beginning of that assignment, I noticed how my feelings of joy, disappointment, failure, and success would fluctuate on a daily basis, very similar to feelings that contract teachers experience throughout their careers.

My interview for the job was with the second grade teacher, newly pregnant, newly certified, and newly hired just three months earlier. She and I met while her students were at lunch, and we hit it off. I did not get to meet the class and assumed there was no additional information needed, other than it was a *typical* second-grade class (no such thing). She was enthusiastic, very sweet, and wore a pair of rainbow-colored sneakers that she said her female students loved. Ms. Rainbow Sneakers explained she was leaving because she "accidentally" became pregnant and felt badly about having to go on maternity leave after just being hired for her first teaching job ever.

We ended the interview on an encouraging note about my getting the job, but she said she just needed to run things by her administrator first and would let me know in the next two days. I did find it strange that she was the only one interviewing me, absent of any administrators, parents, or co-teachers. This is not the way it usually works and most likely would not happen like this today.

Ms. Rainbow Sneakers called me two days later with the offer to take the job. We talked a bit and then she added, "Oh, by the way, this class is a bilingual second-grade class." I mentioned that I was not bilingual. I remember her disappointment at first, then, after she thought about it more, said it might not be an "issue" after all. "Let me talk to my principal, and I think it should be okay for the six to eight weeks you would be here," she said.

Turns out it was "okay," and I got the job even though I was not fluent in Spanish, had no bilingual credentials, and knew nothing about the nuances of teaching, let alone teaching within a bilingual second-grade classroom. But I knew I would find out soon enough. I had two weeks during which I was on call and ready to go once receiving word that Ms. Rainbow Sneakers was in labor. Sure enough, a week and a half later, I was driving into the city to meet my students for the first time. I was terrified. Upon arrival, the students were sweet and loving. *This isn't so bad*, I thought. They welcomed me immediately, but as we got more comfortable with one another, I soon learned my students were not without numerous academic and social-emotional challenges. My lack of Spanish was the least of my problems in figuring out how to both help these students grow and make that human connection necessary in such a short time.

I decided to keep a journal to write down Spanish words I learned and important information that would be helpful with the students and our classroom schedule. I also had a handbook for quick translations to help with communication. At the beginning, many students were missing their teacher and felt disconnected and unsafe by her sudden departure. The classroom was in disarray, and I went to work in the morning nervous and uncertain, and left in the afternoon feeling the same. I learned that some students had serious emotional and social needs that I had not been made aware of by any staff or the classroom teacher when we discussed important details before her departure. I did not know that second graders were strong enough to throw a chair at you. It was during this job that I learned just how much anger a small child can hold in their bodies and that when unleashed can feel like a verbal and physical explosion felt to the bone. It can shake you so badly, you want to retreat to the nearest bathroom and have a good cry.

It wasn't until my third week that an older and more experienced teacher entered my room at the end of the school day. She was an angel in disguise. "Hi, honey," I remember Ms. Angel saying in a sweet, maternal way. "I just want you to know that we are all so happy you are here. You are doing a great job, and teaching is far from a cake walk, that is for certain. Keep your head up, shoulders back, and just love those students. Just let them feel you care a little, and that will go a long, long way." I thanked her and told her I was struggling in more ways than one. I was questioning my place within the world of teaching in general. I remember her mentioning that she sensed this, hence the reason for the visit. She knew I was not bilingual, and the other teachers were upset about my placement for that reason, but not to worry. "There are three things you need to do to make a difference during your short time here: Earn respect from your students, mean what you say—be true to your word, and connect with these kids and let them know you care."

Soon after that experience, I realized I needed to earn their respect and trust immediately, and those were the top priorities. I learned that once I began building connection, I could do a good job teaching math, reading, and writing to these students. I also learned that not all my colleagues would support me, especially when they realized I was not bilingual but was hired to teach in a bilingual classroom. What really mattered, though, was I surround myself with those people who lifted me up and pushed me in a positive direction. My focus was on my students, and I stopped worrying about what others thought about my placement at the school, even though it was for a limited time. I worked to present a confident person with character, one who cared and established mutual respect. I needed to take care of myself, be rested, well prepared, and avoid any negativity that would distract from my teaching.

  Those second graders taught me valuable lessons in how taking care of myself enabled me to take better care of them. I tried to surround myself with colleagues who were supportive and were willing to collaborate and share ideas for working around the language barrier. I took opportunities to sit outside when the weather permitted and took walks during my lunch break to breathe fresh air and collect my thoughts. I worked on being accountable with my students and following through with consequences and positive reinforcement for good behavior. By teaching and learning through doing, this experience as a substitute classroom teacher in charge of thirty-two second graders for eight weeks during the middle of the school year was invaluable—not including the fact they were thirty-two bilingual second graders. It was more beneficial than hearing about techniques while obtaining my certification in college and observing my co-teacher during my student teaching experience.

Substitute teaching is one of the most valuable tools to prepare you for a real teaching job and one of the best ways to be exposed to dealing with behavioral issues. You can learn and experiment with different types of teaching styles and classroom environments. Subbing made me aware not only of the necessity for establishing human connection with my students but the importance of teaching social and emotional wellness to them.

3
The Power of Playground Observation

"The playground simulates real life and social structures for kids," a colleague once told me while discussing an incident that had just occurred on the school playground during lunch. "It is the place where everything goes down."

Playground observation is a powerful tool to help teachers understand the social and emotional wellness needs of their students. In "The Educational Role of Recess," researchers Anthony D. Pellegrini and Carl D. Glickman write: "Recess is a rich opportunity for assessment of social development through informal observations. Teachers observing children on the playground during recess can assess peer popularity, a proven predictor of school adjustment" (*Playground*, 1989, 68: 23–24). *Popularity* here does not mean being "popular" in the sense that children of all ages use the word, but rather whether the child fits in with others, chooses to interact with peers, and is confident with peer relationships outside the classroom.

It took about five years of teaching for me to understand and see the benefits of the playground as a useful tool of observation to help students. I had many students come in from the playground after lunch distraught, disturbed, and frustrated, but I had no idea why. Kids were fighting, sorting out arguments, dealing with disappointments, and with no way to feel supported or have any closure before transitioning back to academics and school. I had not recognized that playground time was even more important for children socially than the physical release of energy this activity provided.

During games and group activities, students are constantly discovering and negotiating with their peers and friends. Certain kids may show themselves as leaders on the playground while displaying the opposite behavior among their peers in the classroom. Some students remain neutral—playing with a few kids and enjoying periodic solitude from time to time. Kids who are leaders in the classroom may become followers when thrust into the outside fenced domain. The playground may also reveal potential problems in students that may show up in or outside the classroom.

During recess, children are faced with choices in their interactions. They can choose to be alone or with others. Some may prefer to hang around the adult supervisor. They may experience rejection or inclusion. What happens on the elementary school playground mimics real life situations for students.

Part of a teacher preparation program should be to watch elementary kids at any grade level on the playground during lunch recess. The playground is a training ground for the development of gender roles and the preparation for adulthood, including navigating essential lessons in sharing, rejection, compassion, independence, and resolving conflicts. Elementary-aged children are the most malleable because they are at the crucial stage when their brain is still forming.

Experienced teachers are aware of the strong evidence in the power of informal observation within the classroom, namely, identifying triggers or events that lead to positive or problem behaviors. Continual observations and data collection can then be used to develop formal plans or programs as needed. Just as informal observation within the classroom can help children excel, the same holds true with conducting these observations during playground time.

I would also encourage teachers to enhance their professional relationships with para-educators on duty for recess, as they can provide very helpful insights. These individuals have a difficult job managing the playground in all types of weather and should be valued for their efforts. Your collaboration with them can prove invaluable, with extra eyes going to support students in and out of the classroom.

Recording and Communicating Playground Observations

Developing a system of recording playground observations can help teachers determine a child's strengths and needs. This data is useful for referencing during parent conferences and phone calls. It makes a big difference to parents when you can share your observations, whether good or bad, and shows that you really care about the success of your students. It also helps "soothe" parents who consistently question and want to discuss their child's social needs, relationships at school, or other concerns. When parents have adequate feedback, it may reaffirm or contradict what they originally believed about their child. I also find the data helpful in showing students their strengths and improvements, plus areas students can improve upon.

Teachers, whether veteran, novice, or somewhere in

between, as well as administrators and school counselors, can benefit from trying out this type of informal observation with students.

The following are suggestions for recording playground observations and communicating findings with parents and students.

1. You might start with observing one child for a couple of weeks, once a week. Or perhaps consider conducting ten- to twenty-minute observations of one small group of students once or twice a week. Start with a group you think would benefit most, and jot their names on paper or in a notebook. Structure observations how it would be most beneficial for you and students being observed. It may take a little while to find a system that is doable and makes sense for you. Observations can be flexible and many ways to make work. Teachers can try and incorporate during recess duty from time to time.
2. Observe students during times when they can't see you. Though I enjoyed having students come over

to me on the playground to say hi and give hugs, sometimes that would make it difficult to document and focus. It may not always be possible, but try and find a quiet spot that benefits quality observing for a short period of time.

3. Note the date and time of day for each playground observation. Certain times of the day might be more difficult for certain students to be calm and engaged in the classroom. It would be interesting to see if playground behavior has any influence on classroom behavior observed.

4. Note behavior patterns, consistencies, and surprises.

5. Note and consider mindful activities that ground students, calm energy, and refocus them for academic and collaborative work, aiding in the transition from outside to inside. Playground observations could aid in finding the most appropriate transition activities to use with a few students at times, or with all.

6. Type up your notes and have one observation ready for parent conferences. Have more than one observation for students who would benefit, and plan to shed light on any extreme problem

behaviors being exhibited on the playground, or in class. Always try to include positive feedback, which can change your dynamic with parents from teacher to team player.

7. Let a student know you have some observations you would like to share with their parent(s). Share your observation with the student *before* sharing it with their parents to build one-on-one trust and human connection. This is a good time to discuss a concern, ask a question, or point out something positive you have noticed. It is always good to ask permission from the student before sharing your observation. If the student refuses, I would honor that request, but also dig deeper to find out why. This demonstrates respect for your student and concern for their well-being.

Turning Playground Problems into Positives

Recess is a time when "things fall apart" socially and are then brought back into the classroom. I often witnessed students enter the classroom crying from a fight outside, an episode of "So-and-So hit someone with a ball in the face," and much more.

Observation can help calm and smooth the sometimes tricky transition from recess to the classroom. Observation allows for positive "I notice" or "I really liked how" comments from teachers to surface: "I noticed how Ryan was really kind by including Lucy in the game at recess today. He noticed she had been wanting to play for a while now." "I really liked how helpful Sarah was on the playground at lunch helping Johnny off the swing. She is so cooperative in reading group too." It also helps to have students generate positive comments to put up in the classroom (on poster board or colorful sticky notes) of how students are making a positive difference on the playground.

This can be an extension of service learning outside the classroom and part of improving the whole school community as well. An example of a positive student comment: "I noticed how Ryan ran hard and let off steam during recess, and now he is ready to focus and get down to business with learning math."

Playground Observations Help Teachers, Parents, and Students

Observations on the playground can help shed light for some parents and give more to the whole picture of who their child is at school. Children can act very different at home than they do at school, and any additional observations can help teachers and parents with action plans to help students succeed. Involving the student in putting together a plan for programming ensures they will be more vested in seeing it through.

When kids asked me what I was doing on the playground, I would say that I was getting fresh air and enjoying the sunshine break from the indoors. I also would say that I was outside to "check things out" and see "what is happening out here, just curious." One student remarked that I "was spying on students on the playground." I let her know that I was learning from kids so I could be a better teacher in the classroom.

Over time, I developed a saying for playground observation of students that I shared with colleagues: "Time spent there can save time here." The time I spent observing actually saved time problem solving or dealing with students displaying acting-out behaviors. This time was saved because I had more knowledge of where the behavior was coming from and could address it head-on. I could talk to students about what I noticed on the playground and give them honest feedback. Just having them know I was taking the time to watch them made a huge difference. I also noticed that certain students lessened their negative behaviors in the classroom as a result of my spending time teaching and empowering them to sort out difficulties on the playground and letting them generate ideas on how to do that. Less time spent on post playground disruption and conflict in the classroom equals more time for learning.

If we want to prepare our students, the best way possible for the twenty-first century, we need to incorporate more time for observation, including their behavior on the playground. It can be easy for busy teachers to think, *That's not my job* or *That is So-and-So's job*, but many teachers already take it upon themselves to do tasks above and beyond what their job description says. But more importantly, we know that teachers can learn vital things about students through observation.

What is noticed on the playground can be an indicator of violent or aggressive behavior down the road.

It can also show positive behaviors that do not appear within the classroom walls. Observation is crucial to identifying social skills that need to be taught for a healthy self-concept and interacting with others.

It is the teacher's job to prepare and cultivate human connection both within and outside of the classroom. Doing so also improves the school experience for parents, knowing that teachers are working all angles to serve the best interest of their students.

Section II
Finding Teacher Wellness

"Children are still more vibrationally imbued with that feeling of passion and joys--and that is what this work is about.
It's to assist you in returning to the natural state of Well Being."

—Esther (Abraham) Hicks, from a talk in San Rafael, CA, February 21, 2004

4
Why Teacher Wellness?

What does it mean to be well and feel well as an educator? The purpose of teacher wellness is to maintain your energy and protect it in order to put your best self in front of students and colleagues. Teachers who practice regular self-care feel innovative to take risks and refine best practices.

While I was in teacher preparation programs, there was never any mention of what we as teachers could do to take care of ourselves and increase our meaningful longevity within the profession. By "meaningful," I mean benefiting from learning and growing within the school environment rather than just counting down the days or barely hanging on until retirement comes.

Forty to fifty percent of teachers leave the classroom within the first five years of their career. I could write about the extensive research, statistics, and reasons why teachers leave their posts every year, and why nearly half of individuals who pursue undergraduate teacher-training programs never enter the profession at all, but that is not the focus of this book. Rather, I am writing in support of teachers and offering suggestions for maintaining energy and excitement throughout one's profession.

Teacher "effectiveness" is at the forefront of the education reform movement: effectiveness as to how students are receiving information and learning from teachers, what teachers are not doing so well and why, and how students are struggling as a result. I want to focus on what *ingredients* can help and enhance teachers to be effective.

Teacher effectiveness is related to taking care of ourselves and in turn providing the best care and nurturing for our students. Promoting teacher self-care in relation to effectiveness is a positive direction in boosting educational best practices and keeping teachers feeling energized and innovative. Many teachers with more than two decades in the profession continue to love their job, stay fresh, and make a huge difference for young people. For every teacher who leaves, I hope there are just as many enthusiastic and promising individuals considering entering the profession!

Most corporate jobs have team-building consultants to guide individuals toward increased productivity and efficiency in business, but teaching is not a business. It is a very different profession and one that impacts young people's lives and futures. Teaching even has certain challenges that can steer people away from wanting to venture into such work in the first place. It can be difficult to find articles and materials that focus on the positive aspects of the job and the teachers who are successful and why. Instead, we often hear about teachers who are criticized for their lack of preparation, teachers who are labeled ineffective, and those made to feel powerless in the bureaucracy of public education.

Though some schools do not empower teachers to believe their voice counts, there are places, which I will discuss later, that respect and value teachers right up there with doctors and lawyers. I have met teachers in schools and programs where they have a say and are very respected by their administration and parent groups. But in order for their "voice" to count on a large scale, there needs to be a shift in beliefs and actions, and teachers need to replace the complaining with being a positive part of the solution.

Believing that your voice does matter and that you are in an empowered line of work can shift your perspective. It is also true that believing the opposite is draining and depletes precious energy that could be saved for teaching students. Teaching does have its obstacles, like any profession. Yet there are ways to approach these obstacles in a positive light, which will keep you refreshed, feeling empowered and well.

Teacher Wellness Suggestions:

Move Schools Every Five Years
A mentor teacher once said to me that a teacher should move schools every five years to stay fresh and current, work in a different environment, meet new colleagues, work with different administrative leadership, and teach a new group of students. She believed that moving schools, even changing grade levels, pushes a teacher to be flexible and prevents feeling stagnant in the job. New challenges can create new perspectives and approaches to add to the best practices toolbox. A move forces growth. Change is good.

Exercise the "Voice" Muscle

Teachers do have a say, and their voice does count. But the voice needs to be positive and part of the solution. Start using this mindset and believing in the impact it can have.

I have known lots of "squeaky wheels" in education who complain about their current situation. They are heard by others but ineffective because complaining only makes them part of the problem.

Honestly, it took me awhile to realize how important it is to stop complaining! Once I figured out how my lack of teaching happiness was directly correlated to my increased focus on what I perceived as negative aspects of my job, I made a change. I was being lazy and not doing the work to find a solution. Complaining is easy, but finding a solution starts with pivoting the mindset and creating change from the ground up.

What ideas can you come up with to improve or change a situation? What action can you take now to formulate an action for the future?

Believe You Are in Control of Your Classroom

You are in charge. Your fellow teacher "neighbor" next door is in charge of their room, not yours. Your assistant administrator and your principal are not in control of your classroom either. You have unlimited power to create useful and entertaining lessons that stimulate eager minds with active learning and inquiry-based learning models. You can uplift young individuals and inspire them to be their best selves! You have the ability to be a role model for other teachers.

Good teaching is like "paying it forward." As with kindness, good teaching is contagious and can spread like wildfire, inspiring one, then three, then six, then twelve—the possibilities are endless!

Trust Your Intuition

Like many teachers, I had feelings throughout my career that something was really wrong with one of my students—I mean really off, not right, really not right. I learned to trust my intuition, and when I did, I was spot-on. In one case, I suspected that a student was experiencing sexual abuse at the hands of a stepfather. After discovering the details in a journal entry the student made available just for my eyes only (she left if on my desk with a note before going to lunch), my suspicions were confirmed, unfortunately.

Always trust your intuition and gut feelings. Doing so will serve you and your students well.

Use Meditation to Enhance Mindfulness

In the chaos of what teaching brings every day, it is important that you stay clear-headed, nonreactive, and balanced. Beginning the day with a meditation practice can help you feel grounded, even before exercise or while waiting for the coffee to brew.

Teachers get up early and are at school early to prep, but carving out time (you can do it!) to quiet the mind by focusing on your breath, a mantra, or perhaps a visualization can provide notable results in how you will approach situations and people throughout the day. Little meditation breaks throughout the day can also help you clear your head and rejuvenate. While students are at P.E., art, music, or lunch, there are chances to sit quietly and peacefully in your classroom for ten minutes or so. Turn off the light so it appears you are out of the room, and find a comfortable place to sit.

Meditation allows clarity to emerge in difficult situations and opens the mind enough to see solutions. Even just standing up and stretching can be a game changer when feeling frustration or irritation with a situation.

Avoid Negative Spaces, Find Positive Places!
When I taught, teacher's lounges were often the last bastion of the burned out or bummed out. Do not surround yourself with colleagues who complain day after day about anything and everything having to do with school—a specific student's behavior, an administrative decision, a school activity, and more. Routinely immersing yourself in this environment will certainly drain your energy and only feed into the negativity of others.

Consider setting up a lunch group that meets in different classrooms each week to discuss wins and challenges. Or maybe other teachers would join you in a lunch walking group outside to get exercise and fresh air. Perhaps you could start a book club where you discuss different books related to improving teaching practices and share feedback with colleagues. The possibilities are endless!

Write to Feel Right: Keep a Journal

Keeping a journal is a constructive and positive strategy to release the events of the day and help you feel better and re-energized. You can also use a journal to track details and events and observe progress with students or parents over the course of your teaching. I liked to record positive quotes or affirmations for reflection when necessary.

It is important to remind yourself of all the good work you are doing as a teacher. Use your journal to note examples of these things. If you are nervous before a meeting, conversation, or parent conference, or simply having a rough day, revisit some positive entries about your efforts, which should help provide perspective and confidence.

Find Your Peeps

Find those people who uplift rather than submerge. Try to surround yourself with like-minded people and colleagues, whether they are administrators, mentor teachers, social workers/counselors, or others. Many parents of your students can be some of your greatest allies and support systems in times of need. The more you work with parents (instead of against them), the better for your students . . . and you!

Start a Righteous Revolution
Be the change you want to see in your school and for your students! Be righteous and teach students how they can righteously revolt with acts of kindness. Reduce the negativity. Think of creative ways to leave positive messages throughout school. Having students do this too can shift the school vibration.

A few years ago while working within a large K-8 school, I noticed a whiteboard situated for everyone to see while in the teacher workroom and visible when en route to the teacher's lounge. This whiteboard was apparent to all teachers and staff working in the room, making copies, laminating, or cutting paper with the "Guillotine" (a giant paper chopper, or industrial-size paper cutter, for those unfamiliar —I love the name). Anyone and everyone (including students and parents) who entered this workroom would surely notice what was on the whiteboard. Also, this workroom was connected to the teacher's lounge, of all places.

It was in early October, still fresh into the beginning of the school year, when someone had started writing in large print a "countdown" of sorts for everyone to see. Each item in the list showed the number of days until teachers would have time off from the students:

- Days till Thanksgiving break
- Days till Christmas break
- Days till spring break
- Days till end of school year
- Actual workdays left in school year
- Actual workdays with students

You get the gist. A lot of time and effort was spent doing the math to determine how many days remained till the next opportunity to have time off from work. This is an example of what does not improve the psyche of the school. I was surprised that our principal did not make a point to erase the whiteboard, let alone discuss its negative message during a staff meeting. It is crucial that the school community and physical environment represent positivity and reflect messages of hope and support.

Instead of promoting negativity, teachers can initiate an uplifting wave of consciousness. Anonymous whiteboards in the workroom, classroom, or elsewhere in the school could convey upbeat, encouraging, empowering messages. Teachers, students, administrators, and staff could contribute.

Be Kind to Support Staff

It is a good rule of thumb to be kind to everyone in the work environment, of course, but don't overlook the hard work and importance of your co-workers in the front office, cafeteria, and on the janitorial staff. Their jobs are not easy, and they are the backbone to keeping everything in the school running smoothly. Your relationship with these individuals will support you in ways you did not even know existed.

The office staff can fend off a disgruntled parent until you are available, assist in setting up special events or presentations for your classroom, and give you a heads-up before a practice fire drill is coming so you can be prepared.

At one school, my fifth-grade students organized jobs within the classroom to help with various tasks, including keeping our space tidy. As part of this effort, my custodian offered to help me move furniture into the classroom. My class also suggested that once a week, five students would leave ten minutes early to help the custodian set up in the lunchroom for the onslaught of children coming in to eat. The students rotated this job weekly throughout the classroom. The lunch staff greatly appreciated the students' efforts to work together for the betterment of our school.

      This particular custodian developed a wonderful bond with a male student of mine who traveled to school by himself each day, taking the bus an hour plus both ways, just so he could be at our school. At the end of the school day, the custodian accompanied my student to the public bus stop in front of the school and made sure he safely boarded the bus. When this student sometimes arrived an hour plus before school started, we (custodian and myself) created jobs for him to do around the school and got permission for him to be in the building before school started. My student took pride in these jobs and better this than sitting outside alone, unattended and in what would be freezing cold temperatures at times.

* * *

Taking care of yourself increases not only your well-being but your effectiveness as a teacher. Surround yourself with meaningful support systems. Change schools to recharge and stimulate creativity. Nurture your relationship with co-workers. Develop certain rituals and positive habits that promote self-care.

Finding your teacher voice and feeling empowered from self-care will allow you to take a stand and begin saying no to certain conventions within the profession that do not serve schools, teachers, or students well. Modeling taking care of yourself sends a positive message that will help students want to do the same. If teachers do not take a stand and fight for their convictions, how can students be expected to? Part of this empowerment is knowing what is within your control and what is out of your control and feeling empowered enough to make the best of the difficult issues you will face.

5

Maintaining Wellness
"Control Versus No Control" Within the
Public Education System

I have mentioned previously that the teacher is the one in control of the classroom culture and has the ability to create magic within. Articles and media discussions around the biggest challenges facing public schools today often paint a picture of these challenges as being overpowering or too large for a teacher to have any control over. Difficult issues certainly exist within public education, yet every person in the role of teacher can help alleviate them or has the power to make the best of the circumstances. The only catch is in believing this is possible.

      This chapter looks at three factors within the public education system that impact you but may be out of your control to change: classroom size, poverty, and family environments. What you do have control over is how you choose to approach them.

Classroom Size

I have had classrooms in small spaces intended to accommodate thirty-five or more growing fifth graders who could have been mistaken for middle-schoolers. I asked my students what they thought we could do to help create more space. They decided that teams of five could draw up plans to rearrange the room, including a map of the tables, desks, a couch, and two beanbag chairs. Students voted on the design they liked best but decided that at the beginning of each month, they would switch the arrangement again so that every design plan could be used at some point, which would enable students to sit next to different people and refresh the energy of the room.

      I decided to take the design process further and turn it into a community building activity. I took the map we would follow for a particular month and added my own tweaks without taking away from the original plan. I incorporated student needs into the plan, like "Table arrangements should be boy/girl" or "You need to sit next to someone you have never sat by before." I gave my students clear, high expectations, and it was amazing how they met them every time. I also gave them a time limit to begin the "remodel" and once required them to do it without talking, allowing only nonverbal cues and writing notes. It was so interesting to stand to the side, not get involved, and allow them to resolve any issues on their own. Very empowering for everyone.

Each new arrangement was more fluid than the last. Students were committed to making each remodel work and took ownership in solving any difficulties along the way.

I also became very creative with using hall space and negotiated extra space with our librarian for kids who were more independent and could work well without constant supervision. Those kids appreciated the trust and privilege given and rose to the occasion—meeting the high expectations set forth.

Ultimately, we had more than enough space and respected the space we had created together.

Being creative and trusting your instincts allows for taking risks to find solutions that work. Students are also having this modeled for them and are learning from your intention to make something better for everyone.

Poverty

Poverty is not something teachers can change, but we can change how we approach students below the poverty level who enter our domain. Educating oneself on students' basic needs is the best start. Are they hungry most of the time? Are they tired? Can we find ways to help with keeping extra snacks on hand in our classroom? Can we allow a child to have space to rest or take a time-out if needed (maybe at lunch or during recess)?

Home visits were one of the most valuable routines I instituted when I first began teaching. I have worked in classrooms where the majority of students have been below the poverty line. It requires some extra time and super creative approaches to keep students excited and motivated to be there. Teachers can make a huge difference in helping students see a different way possible than the one to which they are accustomed. Anything is possible and students need to be told this at school, especially at school.

Family Environments

I had a discussion with a family member who stated, "Parents should be responsible for emotional and social wellness of children, not the teacher." I explained to this wise family member that many others believe this philosophy too. Though this approach might have been acceptable in the traditional model of education dating back to the 1950s, twenty-first-century teaching requires daily social and emotional skills activities and enrichment just like daily math, reading, and writing instruction. The reality is, family environments may or may not provide social skills and respectful modeling of how to treat others, what is acceptable and unacceptable touch, managing feelings in a healthy manner, and taking responsibility for one's actions.

6
Being Empowered

Be well. Feel empowered.

My mother sent me an e-mail with a link to the documentary called *Billions in Change*. The film focuses on Manoj Bhargava, a businessman and philanthropist who invented the popular 5-Hour Energy drink. Many of you have probably heard of it and maybe even tried it.

Bhargava pledged to donate ninety-nine percent of his roughly four billion dollars of net worth to solving the world's most pressing problems. Now, the point of me sharing this with you is not because I am promoting the product, but because I was struck with something Bhargava said in the film. Bhargava explained that when someone approaches him with a product idea, he asks them two questions: The first question is, "Is it useful?" and if it is not useful, he asks, "Is it entertaining?" If the product developer says no to both, there is only one option left and that is for Bhargava to respond, "Not useful." I immediately related this to Western educational systems and teaching. Next time you teach a lesson, ask yourself, *will this information be useful for my students? Will it at least be entertaining?* If you hear a resounding *NO,* perhaps reconsider teaching what will be more beneficial for most, if not everyone in your classroom.

Bhargava also states, "The world is facing some huge problems and there's a lot of talk about how to solve them." He mentions how his talking does not reduce pollution, grow food, or heal the sick. That takes doing. This also parallels our current public education system and the initiative by teachers to begin and continue doing what it takes for students to be successful. Although Bhargava does not mention education, I believe his inspirational message applies.

Education has been facing huge problems for a while now, and I call upon teachers to be the beginning momentum toward fixing these problems. There is a lot of talk from people foreign to the realities of public school life, such as politicians and those in corporate America, who subscribe to knowing how to fix these problems but who alone cannot make the changes necessary. However, it is our teachers who have an intimate understanding of the complex challenges and are in a position of spearheading solutions needed—especially in the students' formative years of early childhood and elementary school.

I have spent hours reading material that discusses why academic teaching alone does not help kids excel in life, nor does it reduce the violence in schools. The ever-increasing barrage of standardized testing and useless curricula being fed to students is not the answer either.

Teachers are doers who know what it takes to create magic for kids inside the classroom and active learning that goes beyond the classroom and out into the world. Teachers also know that a partnership with parents is needed to support efforts that will force change within the infrastructure, from the classroom outward. It doesn't take much more than one person who cares an awful lot to set in motion the kind of education we need to affect many students and change lives. It is the social and emotional wellness teaching piece that is so crucial but missing throughout many public schools.

It is you, the teacher, who will make the difference. It is time to take a stand, avoid negative energy in your building, find another school environment if that might work better for you, and begin teaching what will be useful and saying no to the extraneous stuff. At times you may be educating parents along with their children on social and emotional wellness. The time is now for allowing kids to learn creatively without worries of standardized tests and funding. What would happen if you said no to administering a state test? Would you lose your job? Would you really? What is the worst thing that could happen? What if parents and teachers actually got behind a movement changing how we measure accountability in schools in the right direction toward supporting students in moving forward?

Section III
Creating an Effective Teaching Environment

"Everyone who remembers his/her own education remembers teachers……..the teacher is the heart of the educational system."

—Sidney Hook (1902–1989), American philosopher

7

Teacher Effectiveness: Making Learning Useful and Entertaining

Effective educators provide a learning environment where each student can learn and receive support for their achievements. These teachers find resources and devise lessons and activities that contribute not only to their students' learning but also to their self-esteem and social skills.

Teacher effectiveness depends on many factors. Among the most important: creating a learning environment that is both useful and entertaining in order to maximize student engagement, growth, and success for life.

Making Learning Useful and Entertaining

To be clear, kids should learn to read, write, do math, and develop other valuable skills. But at the same time, teachers should examine how useful and entertaining their teaching is and whether they are focusing purely on content. For content to be meaningful to students, teachers must explain why and how the content applies to real life.

It took me a long time to figure out that having my students memorize content and then spew it out for a test resulted in most of that memorized spew being soon forgotten. Also, sending the message to kids that there is only one right answer materializes later as a fear of failure. How, then, do we creatively and innovatively reach kids, like the inspiring educator Rita Pierson did, through academic teaching that builds self-esteem and academic achievement?

I used to think that my highest-achieving students in our academic-oriented system were the most engaged in my teaching. It became apparent to me that this was not true. I came to realize that these students had mastered how to "do school" very well. Those who were disruptive and not achieving in the academic realm were often some of my brightest students and mostly highly creative leaders. I was doing them a huge disservice. It took me by surprise to realize this.

Many of my students who were considered not academic by their parents or previous teachers came into my room feeling already defeated. They had been labeled by the system, so they had gotten the message loud and clear that they would not measure up or be as smart as So-and-So.

Up to this point, I had been a teacher who controlled the classroom and asked all the questions. But I began to see that my students needed to be confident asking questions themselves and that I did not always have to provide an answer to everything—it was okay to leave some questions unanswered and inspire students to keep questioning and discovering answers for themselves. Rather than teaching them there was one right answer, I stopped looking for something specific from my students and allowed them to stay open to possibilities.

As I continued to practice this new teaching approach, one of my graduate professors told me about a position at a nearby elementary school whose mission supported an experiential and active learning model. I was fortunate to be hired and began teaching a four- and fifth-grade split class. I experimented with lessons and activities driven by student interests and goals and was holding students and myself accountable for teaching and learning, letting lots of questions guide instruction. My students and I created a giant "question book," which I received a grant for, in which we filled pages with amazing questions. This was one of my most prized possessions as a teacher—a beautiful, giant book the size of me that spread out as accordion of pages when you opened it. It contained simple questions like, *Why is the sky blue?* and *Why do we have eyebrows?* to *What is the purpose of war?* and *Why don't people stay married?* It was a constant reminder to stay curious in our classroom and it served as a springboard to deeper and more meaningful inquiry.

When using content to teach the skills necessary for real-life math, reading, and writing, it is important to leave room for failure and learning from mistakes. Also, students should have opportunities to collaborate with others and even communicate with students across the globe virtually as part of useful and entertaining education. This simulates professional life and the importance of having social skills and the ability to collaborate.

Some teachers may find it difficult to focus on the useful and entertaining for fear of not obtaining standardized testing results desired by the school or state. This is a dilemma teachers face, and it is only getting worse.

8
Time's a-Wastin': Standardized Testing

Jonathan Kozol rose to fame as an author on urban education. In a lecture at Harvard in 2007, he stated, "Wonderful teachers should never let themselves be drill sergeants for the state." I would add: Wonderful teachers debate whether standardized testing is useful, but there is no debate about it being entertaining. That is a unanimous NO.

I could not agree more with education lecturer Alfie Kohn, who, in his book *The Case Against Standardized Testing: Raising the Scores, Ruining the Schools*, wrote: "Standardized tests can't measure initiative, creativity, imagination, conceptual thinking, curiosity, effort, irony, judgment, commitment, nuance, good will, ethical reflection, or a host of other valuable dispositions and attributes. What they can measure and count are isolated skills, specific facts and functions, the least interesting and least significant aspects of learning" (Portsmouth NH: Heinemann, 2000, pp. 17–18).

Lyndsey Layton, in her article "Study Says Standardized Testing Is Overwhelming Nation's Public

Schools," reported that "a typical student takes 112 mandated standardized tests between pre-kindergarten classes and 12th grade, a new Council of the Great City Schools study found. By contrast, most countries that outperform the United States on international exams test students three times during their school careers" (*The Washington Post*, October 24, 2015).

Fuzzy Math and the Disastrous Path

I loved using the term "fuzzy math" after I first heard it mentioned during the 2000 U.S. presidential election debates. George W. Bush used it in response to some government spending figures that his running mate, Al Gore (the Democratic candidate), referred to. Bush accused Gore of using fuzzy math in his explanation of these figures. In essence, it refers to things that just don't add up. It is like the math that students are expected to know for standardized testing during their formative years of elementary and middle school. But how much of the math state testing requires is actually useful for most students in their future careers and lifestyles? Assessments which evaluate student learning and how that will be valuable for personal and professional real life success is something to consider.

Bush can also be credited with the No Child Left Behind Act, which resulted in fuzzy teaching methods. It never did add up to supporting or strengthening schools, teachers, or students academically, physically, or socially and emotionally during my professional career.

It did not yield any success or close the achievement gap between poor and minority students and their more advantaged peers. Instead, the NCLB created a system that could not bear the weight of a standardized testing machine that engulfed daily teaching methods and caused schools to suffer and sacrifice funding for art, physical education, and music. As a result, many good teachers have been led to believe that there needs to be a sacrifice of good teaching practices for the sake of state funding and job security.

> ### *Fuzzy Math Problem (for Fun of It)*
>
> *Let us say a politician comes along and declares that a one percent cut in income taxes would increase job revenues by twenty-five percent. You could have older students work to prove the politician is not using fuzzy math by coming up with figures and projections that make the politician's case so that the numbers add up, or they could show that the numbers just don't add up.*
>
> *Not only are students learning about fuzzy math and the historical "real life" context in which it was used as a catch phrase, usually used by politicians, but it can also be used to create a fun, useful and entertaining extension math problem. Come up with your own fuzzy math problems for students to solve.*

Not Useful, Not Entertaining

Standardized tests can occur over two to five weeks each year, during which time the potential for useful learning is lost. The situation is the same for those students who opt out.

At one job, I watched students ages eight to fourteen sitting in the library and nodding off because their parents opted out of having their kids take the state-standardized test, which we will call WOTSS (acronym stands for waste-of-time-seriously-slow—please feel free to invent your own acronyms). Our administration had derived a plan where our librarian and assistant principals would make sitting in the library "miserable" (actual word used) for those who opted out but came to school anyway. These students had the option to stay home if they were not taking the test, but realistically, who can manage that? Most parents work and can't afford to take weeks off to stay home with their kids.

For the students sent to the library or another room to wait out the tests, nothing useful is happening for them. They sneak peeks at their cell phones when an adult is not looking, slip friend's notes, or pretend to be heavily into a book as they yawn and slowly lower their head onto the desk before being told to "wake up" by the administrator in charge of "babysitting," as I've heard it called. This is clearly not useful, or entertaining and a waste of valuable time.

As I pondered my own personal mea culpa with administering standardized tests while I was teaching, I realized I had discouraged parents from having students take the test—but quietly and discreetly. I also never taught to the test or was asked to do so at any of the schools I worked at. The old argument that "kids will be taking these tests in high school and further down the road in their schooling career, so it is a good way for them to practice" is lame. Many colleges since 2005 have been making the

SAT or ACT "test optional" and basing admissions decisions on other criteria than standardized test scores. There are 880+ accredited colleges and universities that do not use ACT/SAT scores to admit substantial numbers of students. Since our students have strong B.S. detectors anyway, they will question whether filling in small bubbles and clicking answers on the computer is meaningful to their educational experience.

Opt Out of Standardized Testing

The issues mentioned and implications surrounding standardized testing for schools, teachers, and families are nothing new. But standard tests are not going away anytime soon. What, then, can be done to improve the situation?

FairTest (www.fairtest.org/university/optional) is an online center that promotes information for those teachers interested in developing an "opt out" movement in response to the ever-increasing standardized testing requirements. The group explains the benefits of opting out and why it is a valuable option.

Opting out sends the message that school time should be used for teaching and learning, not testing and test prep. Recall that the average student takes 112 tests between kindergarten and twelfth grade, stealing precious time that could be used for in-depth, engaging learning. However, the current options for opting out are inadequate. In my experience, kids who opt out are left to their own devices, relegated to a designated room or library for long periods until the testing window is over—unless the student opting out is able to stay at home the whole time, which is not the norm, nor the most beneficial option.

Everyone has a right to choose what is best for their kids. Some students actually love taking standardized tests. They love the format and perform really well on each test too. I did not opt out my own children because I felt that having my child sitting in the library being punished for my decision was not the best option, neither was staying home, so I picked what I felt was the lesser evil at the time, taking the test.

Take a Stand

Neither the school district nor the school board has the power to change the state's testing laws. But together, teachers can work together with students and their families to influence school districts and school boards. Starting from the ground up can build momentum:

- Get parents, community members, and students to rally around and rethink options around standardized testing other than being used for measuring school accountability.
- Demand better ways to assess and promote student learning. Standardized tests measure little of what parents and others want our future children to learn and experience in schools. They do not measure creativity, critical thinking, collaboration, leadership, or empathy. What can be developed to measure these other important life skills?
- Protest harmful uses of standardized exams. These tests are frequently used in ways that do not reflect the abilities of students of color, English language learners, children with disabilities, and low-income youth. Many other students with test anxiety do not test well.
- Please, do not teach to the test. You know what is best.
- Find better options for students opting out of standardized test taking.

Each brave teacher who has taken a stand against

administering state testing, and has been brave enough to speak out against the testing, mentions ethics, good conscience and integrity as their primary reasons for doing so. I know unions support teachers in making these decisions, and even though I was never a union member, job security should not be an issue.

I have read about brave teachers from Seattle to Chicago, who have refused to allow their students to take standardized tests, from MAP to CSAP (acronym rhymes with TRAP). Superintendents have even threatened teachers with sanctions for their refusal to follow this path when the teachers are actually doing what is best for their students. Government officials need to rewrite Pink Floyd's ballad and "leave those teachers alone!" with regard to state testing.

In my experience and observation, it is very difficult to fire teachers, especially the not-so-good tenured ones, and a process that I have witnessed some principals (displaying poor leadership) avoid at all costs. Also, when I was interviewing for my teaching jobs, I was never asked the question, "Will you promise to administer the [fill in the blank] state test" as part of the hiring process? I was instead asked meaningful interview questions, like, how would I differentiate instruction, work and collaborate with colleagues, and problem-solve serious behavioral issues that may arise in the classroom? Let's leave "No Child Left Behind" behind once and for all and work toward every teacher helping every student find their success.

9
Mindful Classroom Management

A calm and peaceful classroom environment is necessary both for learning to take place and for preserving teachers' energy and passion for instruction. The act of disciplining students can be draining, so it is important that teachers create a classroom community built on human connection, with clear behavioral expectations, as well as one that holds students accountable and helps them understand how their actions affect others.

There are many discipline models for teachers to draw from, but I recommend developing a model that works best for you and keeps you mindful, balanced, and moving forward. Each teacher, class, subject, and situation is different. No approach will fit every situation. Managing yourself well with ongoing self-care will transfer to students. Overreacting and yelling out of frustration and despair will result in a disruptive and chaotic room.

I have seen teachers who consistently, year after year, struggle with discipline problems in their rooms. I have also observed teachers who seem to manage this part of their job effortlessly, and people entering the room feel that calm energy. Some teachers blame ineffective classroom management and disruptions on their students. A common sentiment among teachers is, "Students these days possess the inability to be attentive." I wonder how attentive and present these teachers are with their students.

There will always be classrooms during your career that are more difficult to manage than others—this is for certain. But truthfully, you have the creative ability to take control and help change a situation. It may take time, and some trial and error, but it is within your power and ability. It's important to recognize that.

This chapter offers classroom management suggestions intended to help align you with the goals of wellness for both you and your students while creating that peaceful environment that you both will look forward to coming to every day.

Classroom Management Tips

Do Not Punish the Entire Class
Hold individual students accountable rather than punish the whole class for the behavior of one or two students. Though punishing the entire class is a common technique,

experience has taught me that it can alienate and cause deep resentment among many students, especially those you feel are the most well behaved. Student B.S. detectors are acutely attuned to a sense of fairness; if teachers are unfair, the human connection of respect and trust teachers have worked hard to build can be damaged.

Develop Positive Consequences

Develop "rules" around positive consequences for desirable behavior exhibited in the classroom. I have found that students enjoy and feel empowered by determining the actions that warrant these positive consequences, or rewards. It is good teaching to point out which behaviors have a positive effect on others and why—and to encourage a positive learning environment within the classroom. As good teachers, we know the power of positive reinforcement.

Pay Attention to the Mirror and Ripple Effect

It took me a while to realize that how I felt and how I felt about my students became manifested in reality. Students can morph into the child you believe them to be—good or bad. If I was feeling negative, frustrated, anxious, worried, or discouraged, my students would invariably mirror and reflect this behavior back to me. I also became acutely aware that discussing aloud an example of a student's positive behavior could create a ripple effect in the room, resulting in a positive change of behavior in others.

Observe how you feel, and notice what is happening in the classroom. Ask yourself if there is any correlation between what is happening between and among students with what is happening within you. Where we focus our attention most often becomes reality.

Avoid Referring Students for Disciplinary Action
Do not send students to the principal, assistant principal, or out in the hallway to sit unattended with nothing to do other than pick mud off their shoes. Even if you send them out with work to do, it will most likely not get done optimally.

I find it best to avoid referring students altogether, a practice that is particularly important for new teachers to learn early on. The only exceptions would be when a student is demonstrating dangerous or harmful behavior. Most of the time, though, in about ninety percent of the cases I observed during my professional career, students were being referred for reasons other than these.

The act of referring sends the message to students that you are unable to handle them on your own—and that you do not care enough to do so. It weakens your influence, your relevance, and your leadership presence. Most importantly, it can negatively impact your self-confidence in dealing with challenges, which is part of the job.

I have also noticed that sending kids away when things get tough makes it difficult for teachers to hold students accountable and follow through. After all, the administrator was not present when whatever occurred incited the referral in the first place. Plus, the administrator does not have the day-to-day human connection with your students that you have worked so hard to establish. Principals and assistant principals are too busy and overloaded as it is with going beyond job requirements to take on your disciplinary role too. And last but not least, the student who was sent out will eventually be returning to the classroom in no time. That is for sure. The only difference is that they will know you are unable to handle and manage challenging behaviors on your own, which only increases the likelihood of future misbehavior.

Embrace the Challenge

Challenge yourself to be the ultimate authority of your classroom. Take responsibility for your behavior and the behavior of your students. Not only will you feel empowered, more confident, and earn greater respect and influence with students, but students will feel that you care enough to be there through the good and the bad. You will also be modeling for students that they too are capable of handling real-life difficult situations and can find resolutions. The best part is, the classroom will be filled with less misbehavior as a result.

Shift Attention to the Positive

Being deliberate and observing your attention throughout the school day, both within and outside the classroom, will enable you to respond skillfully to situations and in turn will help elicit a favorable response from your students. Start each day being mindful and be aware of how this awareness affects student behavior and the behavior of others.

Take a student who is causing lots of conflict and disruptions on a regular basis, or a colleague, or even a parent who is creating obstacles. Focus on the positive aspects of this person (or situation) and shift the attention from worry and frustration to a concentrated release of the negatives. The intention of the attention is to see the relationship of you and this person (or situation) changing for the better—for all involved.

I had this happen with a challenging parent of a student of mine. I loved and cared for this student, who was really struggling academically in reading, writing, and math when he entered my fourth-grade classroom. The parent was merely looking out for her only son and trying to make sure he was getting all his needs met the best way possible, from her perspective.

At first, I used excuses to dismiss her because I perceived her requests negatively. In time, I began to realize that we both really wanted the same things for her son—to feel nurtured, loved, and happy at school. So I started to change how I reacted to her calls and e-mails. I saw us as a team working for this student's best interests together. I saw her in a positive light, a single mom advocating for her son and hoping for the success she had yet to see him experience in the classroom setting.

Over time, things began to change. This mother soon became my greatest ally and support when it came to selecting innovative programs approved by the school district and assigning literature that contained situations he could identify with and learn from ("dangerous truths," as I discuss in chapter 16). I have always remembered her and often think about her son. I am grateful for the lessons they taught me.

10
Social and Emotional Wellness of Students

As discussed earlier, creating human connection between teacher and students allows for a more positive and effective learning environment. In addition to creating human connection, teaching social and emotional wellness to students can also improve academic performance—and much more, as the article "Study Finds Social-Skills Teaching Boosts Academics" by Sarah D. Sparks shows (*Education Week,* February 4, 2011).

Social and emotional learning, or SEL, improves positive attitudes toward oneself and others. Daily lessons in social and emotional wellness increase respect and collaboration among students and reduce disruptions throughout the school day. In addition to helping academic performance, teaching SEL could significantly enhance safety and violence prevention.

Lessons in SEL are more important than any standardized test in gauging whether our students will thrive in their communities. One of the most crucial issues we face in education as we move forward into the twenty-first century is the lack of teaching social and emotional wellness to students at the early childhood and elementary levels. The teaching of social and emotional skills is also important in the upper middle level and high school stages but has to be prominent in early education. Pre-school and elementary students have the gift of having the same teacher throughout the day. These students sometimes see their teacher more in a regular weekday than their actual parents or caregivers.

I remember where I was on April 20, 1999. I was working as a fourth-grade teacher when the horrific massacre occurred at Columbine High School in Littleton, Colorado. I lived a few hours' distance from Columbine, and the event shook me and motivated me to find answers to the growing epidemic of school violence.

I have known many students filled with the kind of sadness, anger, and alienation that Columbine students Dylan Klebold and Eric Harris must have felt. Episodes of school violence have taken many lives since Columbine, yet we do not see an overwhelming demand for teaching students the importance of self-care and emotional and social well-being within our Western society. I find this deeply troubling. Dylan and Eric were not "evil" individuals—they were just not receiving the support they needed within their school environments and probably never did. These students were not products of an educational system that fostered self-esteem and taught skills of how to deal with anger and feelings of isolation. By the time they reached high school, it seemed too late. Both boys had found support in one another, which fueled their like-minded despair.

Columbine offered positive lessons and big takeaway messages from the tragedy: It got teachers to think about teaching tolerance, acceptance, and kindness during the beginning stages of schooling for all children; to offer more outreach and connection programs at schools; and to teach ways to cope and work through feelings of isolation or depression at a younger age and nurture students in addition to teaching them academics.

Teaching self-care to students is the result of taking care of your teacher self, which in turn allows you to teach and take care of your students more effectively and efficiently. It involves finding ways to boost students' self-esteem; implementing approaches that help children with sensory disorders thrive; teaching tolerance and acceptance; and teaching overall body-awareness health. Social and emotional learning for students includes building skills for resolving conflicts, handling tough situations, and developing self-awareness, self-management, resilience, social agility, and responsible decision-making skills. Teaching children these skills early on will be a lifelong gift, affecting students' future lives and how they will work for the betterment of society.

In the article by Sparks cited earlier, Corinne Gregory, president and founder of the Seattle-based schoolwide SEL program SocialSmarts, suggested that the improvement of social skills in her program caused a rise in academic achievement, in part, because educators could teach more efficiently, with calmer, more cooperative students. Gregory noted that some schools participating in the Seattle SocialSmarts program reported increasing students' time on task by more than forty percent. The article also mentioned a 2003 brief by the New York City–based policy-research group Public Agenda, which found teachers reported losing as much as thirty percent of instructional time dealing with behavior problems in class.

One finding ran counter to both the researchers' expectations and prior research: Simple teacher-led SEL programs vastly outperformed multifaceted programs involving schoolwide activities and parent involvement. It comes back to the teacher once again.

Many teachers incorporate social and emotional health into daily teaching practices already. They do a wonderful job of building self-esteem and teach respect and kindness within the classroom. But many do not, and academic teaching and standardized testing overshadows valuable time that needs to be redirected to teaching the standards mentioned in emotional and social wellness curriculums. Also, state health curriculums offer few and confusing standards that are hard to understand and are very broad when it comes to teaching basic social skills, body awareness, establishing appropriate boundaries, respecting our bodies, and keeping our bodies safe. These curriculums across states need to be current, taking into account the influence of technology and social media on young people.

Teaching social and emotional wellness daily—like teachers do with math, reading, and writing—is crucial for not only the academic success of students, but life success. Because educators are not able to assess social skills learned in the same fashion as reading, writing, or math, schools and teachers tend to lean away from focused instruction. However, as mentioned in chapter 3, teachers are able to use observation to assess these skills and notice positive differences in the classroom as a result.

Additionally, students are being socially assessed by their peers on a daily basis in class, on the playground, and outside of school. If children receive positive feedback on these "tests," they are likely to be well liked and happier at school. If not, the opposite is true. I believe failing social tests are more upsetting for students than failing a math or science test—and more important. Social tests are often harder to pass than any academic test too.

In *Building Academic Success on Social and Emotional Learning: What Does the Research Say?* Joseph E. Zins et al. present considerable evidence that schools integrating SEL within their academic mission will be most successful in outcomes (New York: Teachers College Press, 2004). Addressing the social-emotional challenges that interfere with students' connecting to and performing in school is therefore critical. Issues such as discipline, disaffection, lack of commitment, alienation, and dropping out frequently limit success in school or even lead to failure.

Many new professionals entering the teaching force need training in how to address SEL to manage their classrooms more effectively, to teach students better, and to cope successfully with students who are a discipline challenge. Moreover, such training likely will help these teachers manage their own stress more effectively and engage in problem solving more skillfully in their own lives.

Teaching Social and Emotional Skills to Students
Lessons in social and emotional skills, taught through daily practice, will encourage students to work together to improve their skills in the classroom, which will then spread into the school and the community. The goal is for students to be socially adept. Activities like role-playing of real-life scenarios, modeling, inviting community professionals and guest speakers into the classroom to address topics generated by student-driven ideas will help make learning these important life skills relevant and impactful.

Consider the following suggestions to get you started. Aim for setting aside twenty to thirty minutes a day, or an hour three times a week, with special events and guest speakers to reinforce learning.

- **Greeting others.** Whether students are walking down the school hallway or taking their dog for a walk in their neighborhood, making eye contact and offering a simple greeting to others is a must. A simple "Hello" or "How are you?" works, but a smile, the tone of voice, and other gestures are important too. Modeling this behavior in front of students is crucial. I never understood colleagues who would walk right by without any acknowledgement. This does not serve persons well in the world. Let's help kids understand this!
- **Starting a conversation.** This is not easy for many. Starting a conversation, being able to continue it, maintain it, and end it appropriately—these take practice. It is a reciprocal dance knowing when to talk and when to listen. I have worked with many impulsive kiddos who have difficulty knowing when to talk and when to listen—and how not to interrupt. I always used to tell my students to remember to push the "pause button" in a conversation before rushing to get the next word in.
- **Feeling empathy.** Personally and professionally, the ability to feel empathy is what enables one to

really connect with another. Teaching students that by trying to understand what other people are feeling will help them avoid being called self-centered or unkind. We all can find empathy with one another if we really work at it. It is more important than ever.

- **Reading verbal and nonverbal cues.** Teaching students to read social cues is important in directing their conversation and letting them know if they may have upset someone, confused or bored them, or cheered them up. Questions for students to consider: "What is the other person not saying that is giving me clues to how they are feeling?" "What is their facial expression?" "What is their tone of voice?" "Is their body tensing up as I discuss [fill in the topic]?"
- **Listening to others.** Listening to others can be challenging and thus important to teach children at an early age. How children talk to adults is different than how they talk to peers. Teach students that they do not always have to talk or respond. They can wait until when they think someone is done talking and not speak right away. This

communicates that they are listening, that they care, and often the person will continue sharing and will not need or want a response. We all want to feel heard and understood. Listening to others is a gift.

- **Solving problems.** Conflict is an inevitable part of life, so it is essential that students develop confidence at an early age that they can work out issues. All relationships involve negotiating and learning to compromise. Because kids often have disagreements with friends, it is beneficial if they can find a solution that works for both people involved. Good problem-solving skills take practice, and ample opportunities exist in the classroom for role-playing conflict scenarios.

- **Forgiving.** We all make mistakes, and it is important to apologize if we have wronged someone. Sometimes it takes courage to admit a wrongdoing and give a sincere apology. Help students see that it can be harmful to hold onto resentment or anger. It helps us feel freer to forgive and move on, and that includes forgiving ourselves! Students need to know that forgiveness allows them to be healthier and happy!

* * *

In addition to teaching the basic social and emotional skills mentioned above for building the classroom community and nurturing a healthy whole child, four other components are necessary to any social-emotional wellness program for early childhood and elementary school-aged children: building self-esteem; teaching tolerance and acceptance; implementing techniques that support sensory integration within the classroom; and ensuring that students are taught body respect, healthy body awareness, and keeping their bodies safe. Teaching these elements early on will establish the foundation for middle school, high school, and beyond for life.

Section IV
Teaching that Promotes Student Wellness

"Anger is an acid that can do more harm to the vessel in which it is stored than to anything on which it is poured."

—Mark Twain

11

Wellness Without the Labels

Some students have difficulty learning and/or moderating their behavior in and outside of the classroom. In response, teachers may use behavior labels like "ADHD," "disruptive," and "difficult" on a regular basis to describe these students. While it is the job of teachers to help identify why these students are not succeeding academically or socially, there is a growing concern among educators that there is too much labeling without the valid criteria or teacher expertise to correctly identify the condition in question. Although the intention of teachers (and parents) is usually to serve the best interests of the child, the practice of labeling could be providing the opposite results. Moreover, what may be attached to the label is low expectations for student achievement and increased teacher bias.

One of the most detrimental and overused labels given to students by teachers is ADHD, or attention deficit/hyperactivity disorder; take out the hyper part and you have ADD. (I discuss what teachers can do about this in chapter 12.)

In his blog post "DSM-5 Diagnoses in Kids Should Always Be Written in Pencil," Allen Frances, M.D., explains the powerful external factors that have contributed greatly to the extensive mislabeling of kids (www.huffingtonpost.com/allen-frances/dsm5-diagnoses-in-kids-sh_b_12732918.html, October, 31, 2016). He cites two doctors, Juan Vasen and Gisela Untoiglich, who are leaders of the Forum Infancias, an Argentine organization of mental health workers dedicated to the proper diagnosis and treatment of children and adolescents. Vasen and Untoiglich provide reasons why psychiatric diagnosis is much more difficult and uncertain in youngsters and how rampant mislabeling leads to over-medication and unnecessary stigma:

- The roles and behavioral expectations of children and adolescents have changed dramatically throughout history, and also vary dramatically across different societies in the current world. It is not necessarily an indication of mental disorder when a child doesn't fit into societal or educational roles that are recent, constraining, and quite narrowly defined.

- Children and adolescents vary dramatically in the way they develop and in the chronology of their developmental milestones. Individuality and immaturity should not be confused with disease.
- Problems that are really most properly blamed on defects in the educational system are instead often blamed on problems originating in the individual child. We would have many fewer children diagnosed with Attention Deficit Hyperactivity Disorder if class sizes were smaller and schools provided more physical activity recesses for children during the school day.
- Parent and teacher perfectionism, and the desire for bland conformity, has narrowed the range of what is accepted as normal childhood behavior and has devalued diversity. We should not medicalize difference.
- Whenever having a psychiatric diagnosis is made a requirement for obtaining special school services, the rate of diagnosis goes up dramatically and inappropriately. This may give the child a short term educational advantage, but saddles him with

> long term stigma and reduced expectations and risks inappropriate medication prescription. . . .

- It is easy to give a diagnosis, often hard to erase one. "If you choose a wrong name, the child will be forced to walk the wrong road."

When it comes to labeling students, teacher bias has the potential to cause great harm and drastically alter the path of student outcomes in school. It is therefore important for educators to be aware of the effects of labeling on students and how a label given, whether accurate or not, can alter the trajectory of a student being successful academically and socially well-adjusted. Just like "one rule fits all" does not work when it comes to discipline, "one approach fits all" does not work when it comes to the complex task of identifying and meeting the special needs of many students.

Sometimes I wonder if students really understand, or ever ask questions about, the disorders various adults are labeling them—and the implications these labels carry to their personal well-being. I am not saying that real disorders do not exist, yet I wonder whether students might be better served if we approached them with a "clean slate mentality" at the beginning of each year. What if teachers declined to receive a summary of the good, the bad, and the ugly from the previous year's teachers? If teachers were to start with high expectations, what might occur differently?

What if we continued this experiment and did not consult the special education teachers or interventionists right away to hear why So-and-So cannot do all the things we planned for the year? What if we started the year with an equal playing field for all students, where there were no preconceived notions or judgments planted before we got to know each individual student FIRST? Students would respect and respond positively to the idea of our getting to know who they really are. Think of how confidence, feelings of capability and courage could dramatically be altered. More students feeling good and well about who they are as individuals.

I had a phone conversation with a mother of a sixth-grade student who told me that my expectations of her son were unrealistic and could not be met. "You can't expect him to be respectful and be able to work well with others since he is autistic. It is unfair to expect him to do something he WILL NOT be capable of," she said. To this type of thinking, I say that it is unfair NOT to expect all students to be capable of more. My teacher belief is to allow their achievements to be limitless.

As teachers and parents, we have been caught up in the mushrooming popularity of diagnoses and overwhelmed by many descriptions. The list of disorders, for which students are often medicated, is long and pervasive. Diagnoses include "bipolar," "disruptive," "dysthymic," "schizoid," "obsessive-compulsive," and even "existential depression," which is said to be mostly experienced by students identified as "talented and gifted."

The most recent disorder I was introduced to was a "fever" disorder a male student had been diagnosed with while in elementary school. As a sixth grader in my class, he was extremely disruptive, disrespectful, and arrogant. He had recently moved to our school, and when I called his mother to discuss his goals, interests, strength areas, and any other info she felt pertinent for me to know, her response was "none." She was not sure about goals, she said her son had no strengths, and "hopefully he would not be kicked out of school." Actually, that was one goal his mother did have. She also let me know that his getting "fevers" at least once a month might debilitate him and hinder his ability to perform to his best at school. The student told me that the fevers usually came on during math class and he hated math class. Go figure.

Imagine starting the year with a new group of students about whom you hold no preconceived notions and stereotypes. How different that would be for both you and the students if you could actually get to know each student for who they are without being biased by what the previous year's stats or reports showed! There is always the future possibility of considering beginning your teaching year with a clean slate as a stepping stone to building self-esteem with students.

12
Supporting Student Behavior: Rethinking ADHD

All aboard the ADHD train need to rethink and disembark. I have noticed that since I started as a classroom teacher more than two decades ago, an increasing number of children have been labeled by teachers as ADD/ADHD. Differentiating academic instruction is not enough for students who display behavioral challenges. It takes a mental shift in approaching and understanding differences in student behaviors today—behaviors that are symptomatic of social media overload and the ability to ignore authentic human connection by using an electronic device as a shield.

      Mental and emotional disorders are real, though not necessarily cured by medical intervention, and students should not be diagnosed by parents and teachers purely based on classroom behavior—namely, not following the prescribed "law of standards and rules" set up by schools. When kids—ALL kids—have opportunities to study and learn what truly interests them, they have the ability to focus that energy and excitement in a positive way. Freedom to explore subjects that a child is excited about can stimulate better learning and success. Also, kids have very different ways of learning and expressing themselves. Surely, we must allow for more flexibility and tolerance in how they are allowed this in the classroom.

Peter Breggin, a psychiatrist and author of over twenty books, believes ADHD is a misdiagnosis and that teachers are the ones unfortunately doing most of the misdiagnosing. In "A.D.H.D Is a Misdiagnosis" (*New York Times,* October 11, 2011), Dr. Breggin writes that the diagnosis of ADHD, from the 2000 edition of the *Diagnostic and Statistical Manual of Mental Disorders*, is simply a list of behaviors requiring attention in a classroom: hyperactivity ("fidgets," "leaves seat," "talks excessively"); impulsivity ("blurts out answers," "interrupts"); and inattention ("careless mistakes," "easily distractible," "forgetful").

These behaviors, he says, are the spontaneous behaviors of normal children. When these behaviors become age inappropriate, excessive, or disruptive, the potential causes for them are limitless and include boredom, poor teaching, inconsistent discipline at home, tiredness, and underlying physical illness, to name a few. Children who suffer from abuse or stress may also display these behaviors in excess. But by making an ADHD diagnosis, we stop looking for what is really happening. Instead, these children need adults in their lives to give them "improved attention," Dr. Breggin argues.

As mentioned above, unwanted behaviors in the classroom reflect that students are not getting what they need. This bold statement is important for teachers and parents to consider when thinking about ADHD and responding in ways that will support the happiness and well-being of students. A very wise woman I worked with once told me that every behavior exhibited by a child has a reason and purpose behind it. *Every* behavior has some intrinsic reward associated with it—whether it be positive or negative attention seeking.

During my educational career, I observed that certain challenging behaviors, and how to help or prevent them, were collectively similar. Recommendations for students identified as "gifted" to "autistic" to "ADHD" were all basically the same, if not very similar. With all the labels and misdiagnoses out there, it can be easy for teachers to get overwhelmed and confused about how to teach to each one.

What if a student who has been labeled with bipolar disorder is looked upon by the teacher as a student who simply has extreme focus—the focus ranging from extreme positive to negative? It is the teacher's job to direct this center of interest or concentration into positive questioning and discovery. Teachers can help channel this energy and any extreme sensitivities in ways that will create a positive self-concept and benefit the whole child.

> ### *Rethinking Classroom Design*
>
> *I wish I would have explored sensory integration more as a preservice teacher and used this information to help with classroom design and physical structure. Through years of observation and taking steps to understand the extreme sensitivities of students and the subtle messages students receive from their environment, it took me a while to devote more time in creating spaces that would support many student needs.*
>
> *I had couches, rocking chairs, beanbags, tables, desks, standing tables, and inspirational quotes all around the room, and probably still could have done more to ensure greater success of my students—creating an environment that supported more questions than answers and was useful and entertaining!*

The bottom line is that all students want to be cared for, respected, nurtured, and valued, just like their teachers. They want a teacher who takes the time to find out what lights them up, helps them explore, and supports realizing their creativity and academic potential.

As my teacher friends remind me, it is a fallacy to be a "traditional" parent or "traditional" teacher to kids diagnosed with ADHD. "Traditional" in the sense of favoring back-to-basics education and conventional practices that do not take into account the needs of the whole child. In today's ever-changing world, we can't be a traditional teacher to ANY of our students and expect them to thrive in their activities and courses.

Innovative Teaching Approaches for ADHD

Teachers may not agree on why ADHD is such a common diagnosis or whether young children should be prescribed drugs to treat it, but they would likely agree that having students in their classrooms diagnosed with ADHD is the current reality for teachers. Therefore, in working with students displaying the behaviors of ADD/ADHD, teachers need to feel supported and empowered. Consider incorporating the following practices into your teaching on a daily basis.

- **Do not let students use ADHD as an excuse.** Hold HIGH expectations as you would for all students. Also, hold all students accountable, including students with ADHD.
- **Reinforce that students are not victims.** Help students to feel empowered and not fall into victim mode. Students, especially those with ADHD, need to recognize that they are in control of their behavior; their behavior does not control them. This is useful to reinforce to parents too.
- **Provide hands-on activities.** Although not all students with ADHD are kinesthetic learners, many benefit from independent or small-group hands-on activities. You can assess and scale back the students' freedom and include more structure if you observe a need for such.
- **Include movement and regular breaks.** Varying your teaching routines from time to time benefits everyone. Students love to act out scenes from books, role-play great leaders in history, and even stretch and dance a bit. One activity that I found to

be both fun and a great way to build community was to give my students a whole-class challenge, where they were to complete a task (build a tower, rearrange the desks, complete a math mystery), but the only catch was they could not talk. Students had to come up with an alternative mode of communication, like writing, hand gestures, or a "code" language using taps to the arm or leg signaling "yes" or "no." Kids were so creative with what they came up with—it was amazing to be on the fringe and watch. Depending on the class, there would be conflict with some people or groups, but this was a fantastic opportunity to discuss afterward and have students process what happened and why. It was a great learning experience!

- **Incorporate mindful activities in the classroom.** There are many wonderful resources available for teachers and parents on mindfulness for kids. When I left teaching, I was just beginning to explore the possibilities of incorporating mindful activities in my fourth- and fifth-grade classroom. Being mindful brings awareness to the quality of the attention brought to a task. If we are not present and our attention is elsewhere, it is difficult to put forth our best efforts.

Mindful exercises can release tension for students and allow them to get out the wiggles and any distractions before instruction begins. These exercises can also tune kids into their breath and how important breathing is to health and feeling good. Teachers will see how mindful activities can ground and balance out student energy, especially after transitions (recess, lunch). Starting out first thing every morning with a mindful exercise can set a positive tone for the rest of the day.

Practicing Mindfulness: Guided Meditation Using Food:
Try this activity to help ground students, draw attention away from negative thoughts, and settle into learning activities more easily. This is a sensory exercise and good practice in helping kids really focus in on each sense.

Pick a food (I would always use a healthy food, but sometimes treats around Halloween time are fun, if you are brave!). Watermelon is good because most kids like it and it is soothing, especially when it is hot outside. Tell students to imagine that they have a slice of watermelon.

Give them ten minutes to think about the watermelon-the smell, the beautiful color, the touch, the taste-and finally to swallow the fruit. After the ten minutes have passed, have students write down or share aloud their experiences.

You will find that kids notice greater self-awareness and slow down to pay attention to each detail and sensory phase with the watermelon. Students think how their senses are activated, and they find joy in being able to eat this wonderful fruit. This activity can also bring gratitude and appreciation to the forefront of students' minds. Appreciation for being able to eat healthy fruit, how it makes them feel once they eat it, and how fortunate they are to be able to eat this wonderful fruit.

Try it out and experiment with different creative scenarios. A fun option would be to finish the meditation with offering student's real watermelon, if they wanted. I would love to hear other ideas and experiences from teachers and students!

13

Fostering Student Self-Esteem: An Anecdote to Bullying

Part of teaching social and emotional wellness to students is building their self-esteem. If more classroom focus was devoted to teaching social and emotional skills that helped foster self-esteem, the incidences of bullying would lessen. Imagine how valuable this could be in preventing future school tragedies and greater societal issues of hate crimes and ignorance.

A teacher friend mentioned to me that the 2016, U.S. presidential election period had presented excellent opportunities to provide insights and teachable moments on bullying. Although I totally agreed with this person, let's just say I have a hard time with the word "bully." My tendency is to stay away from labels or refer to children using a designation that puts them in a category. I do not feel it is in the best interest of students. In my opinion, the word bully is overused, misunderstood, a word that attaches negativity to someone who is actually just desperately asking for love, support, and improved self-esteem. But for lack of a better word, I will use "bully" in discussing this behavior prevention.

When I read the definition of bully as someone who acts as an "aggressor, tormentor, and intimidator," I thought how it is the person *doing the bullying* who feels tormented, intimidated, emotionally weak, and disconnected from others. The student called bully may even feel more pain than the student toward whom they are acting out.

From time to time, I observed students who others felt were bullies switch "roles" and become the victim, while the victim became the bully. I would see the child labeled "bully" sometimes not so different than the one labeled "victim." It was fascinating to watch and made me wonder, if everyone was feeling self-worth and confidence in their environment, would there be an opportunity to bully, or be bullied?

In looking at bullying from a different perspective, I believe there is no random selection of "victims" or "targets," like some anti-bullying programs suggest—it takes two or more people to make this complex relationship work, including a willingness to participate.

Teachers can help students get more insight into a bullying situation by having students ask themselves these questions:

- Why might this student be coming after me?
- What is *my part* or contribution to creating this situation?
- Do I have something this student may want?
- Are they jealous? IF so, for what reason?
- What gifts do I have to offer that they may be envious of?
- What gifts and positive attributes does this person (the person doing the bullying) possess?
- If I feel really good about myself and full of confidence and contentment, will it be harder to lower my feelings to a level of feeling powerless?

It all comes down to feeling good and not feeling good. The bully does not feel good or strong but powerless and scared. The bully can sniff out who is close to feeling this way too. Will this person the bully has picked allow themselves to be bullied or not? It is a choice. If so, then the relationship starts. If not, the child moves on until they can find a willing participant, and the dance begins.

Teaching must involve ways to handle students' feelings of anger, isolation, frustration, and intolerance that eventually lead to that endpoint on the social-emotional continuum labeled "bully." I use to have a sign in my classroom that stated: "Be POWERFUL, not powerless."

Outside of the school environment, there are factors that influence problem behavior and lower self-esteem. The adults at home may have their own burdens to bare and work through, and they may be modeling behavior that is undesirable and hurtful. We also have abusive situations that kids are living with day to day. Kids naturally gravitate to that which is good. But without that teacher and person of responsibility standing before them—working with them and loving them—how are they supposed to see a different outcome if we are not willing to be the one to deliver the guidance?

At any given time, all students are processing feelings or working through behaviors that may be undesirable or desirable, depending on where they are developmentally and what may be happening outside of school. I propose we incorporate lessons that teach students how to *recognize and handle different emotions*, no matter how extreme; *listen to their inner voice* and trust their intuition in guiding them through difficult decisions now and especially during the teen years; and *settle disagreements* with others peaceably (how to basically get along).

Teaching Self-Esteem for Academic and Life Success

Not only does teaching self-esteem reduce bullying, it increases academic achievement. A dynamic relationship exists between a child's self-esteem and their skill development. Teachers notice that as a student's self-esteem improves, their academic competence increases as well. And as that competence increases, the self-esteem improves in this symbiotic relationship. It is important for a caring and concerned teacher to realize that positive self-esteem is both a prerequisite and a result of academic success.

We as teachers strive to prepare students as future employees who demonstrate "strong communication skills," are "creative and adaptable problem solvers," and will "work well in groups." In doing so, let us recognize that helping to foster students' self-esteem is key to ensuring their chances now and in the future.

Here are some tips to help foster your students' self-esteem:

- **Make students feel important in class.** Give students classroom jobs or responsibilities that help others: answering the class phone, assisting in another classroom, tutoring younger students, and so on. Rituals that celebrate birthdays are always welcomed. Having students acknowledge acts of kindness they have observed or ways their classmates are doing well builds confidence too.
- **Be interested and ask students questions.** Having students fill out questionnaires or converse about activities that they care about shows you care. Also, you or others (students or teachers) may have a resource that can help students pursue their interests deeper, like a book or something else.
- **Celebrate success.** Sending a simple note home or providing a quick shout-out in the classroom can go a long way to boosting a child's self-esteem. Teachers are quick to let parents know when there is a problem, but what about when students are successful at something? Something to think about!

- **Help students see evidence of their progress.** Providing concrete evidence is important in showing students their growth. Using your observations of playground and classroom behavior, you might mention that a student handled a difficult situation in a positive manner for the first time, or they mastered a math problem that had been a struggle earlier in the year.
- **Teach that failure is part of learning.** Help students understand that failure is normal and an important part of learning. Everyone gets disappointed and frustrated from time to time. How we deal with these experiences can make us stronger and more capable. If we fail, it means we are taking risks, and that is key to success in relationships and professional life.
- **Establish the classroom as a safe zone.** All students need to be taught that any behavior that hurts another person physically or psychologically is unacceptable within the classroom (and school). This statement will and must be repeated over and over again, made visually apparent, and reinforced.

Children are always listening (even when they appear not to be) and absorbing this message.

- **Model respect and kindness.** Kids love to role-play scenarios and process these through discussions in small groups, or with the entire class. Consider giving them real-life examples from the playground or classroom and have them thoughtfully work through how each choice made can result in either positive or negative consequences. And remember, teachers are the model who students constantly watch and hear. Be mindful and choose your words and actions carefully!

- **Use literature to teach about being human.** Using stories (reading aloud to students and/or having them read independently) to teach about social and emotional wellness is a winning combination. Not only are you strengthening basic reading and writing skills (comprehension, decoding, and improving vocabulary), you are also strengthening listening and speaking skills (expressing an opinion and sharing information).

Students can relate to and learn from the characters in these stories.

14
Tolerance and Acceptance = Empathy

Is it important for teachers to feel empathy? Yes. Is it important for teachers to teach empathy? Absolutely. Students do not always have this quality, nor do all adults. Empathy takes place in the simple form of being aware of others' feelings and is necessary not only at school but out in the world, even more now than ever.

I knew a teacher who was extremely frustrated with a sixth-grade student. This student was always tuning this teacher out and being disrespectful to her in math classes. The teacher once pulled this student out of the classroom by dragging his chair across the floor in front of all the other students. The student remained in the chair while she did this. Not only is it disturbing to think about how the student must have felt while this was going on but also the message that was being sent to all the other students in the meantime.

On another occasion, this same teacher found herself so frustrated that she held her right hand out in front of her with three middle fingers locked together and remarked to this very same student, "The way you are behaving, you might as well be telling me to read between the lines." Remember, kids are strong B.S. detectors. From my experience, I have learned that kids neither respect nor feel respected by teachers who speak to them as if they were a peer or trying to be cool. If we behave disrespectfully to our students, they will in turn feel like they can be disrespectful back. Respect is a two-way street and must be earned. There are other ways to deal with undesirable behavior.

I understand firsthand the frustration teachers feel with certain students. I have had moments when I wished someone would grant me a "do-over" pass. As a result, I would like to suggest that teachers be acutely aware of their behaviors and reactions to student behaviors that are motivated by trying to illicit a "reaction."

Students listen to the words and observe the actions and behaviors of their teachers. Grouped together, the messages they receive permeate each student in ways that are good, bad, or even ugly. It is therefore vital that teachers model tolerance and acceptance of any gender, sexual identity, and race and present freedom within the classroom for students to explore their own beliefs and ideas.

One student I remember had a particular fondness for using a derogatory word that rhymes with maggot. I strongly feel sick when hearing this word but did not want to be dramatic about my repulsion in front of the whole class when this student used it. I opted instead to approach the situation in a calm manner. It would have been easy for me to send this student out of the room or down to the office, where he would have sat for an hour waiting to talk to our assistant principal. The student would have found either scenario ideal because he was trying to find a way to get out of the work we were doing anyway. I did not want to be someone who would overlook and pretend that I did not hear him each time he uttered this word. Instead, I had him bring his lunch back to the room, while the rest of the class was out to recess. We spent that time together openly and honestly discussing what had happened. More importantly, I wanted to know if my student really understood what *the word* meant and how it felt to be called that. We ate together and calmly discussed the word like two people having a regular conversation. No one was heated, and I learned so much about him as an individual during that talk. The word stopped being uttered and business resumed as usual.

Until . . . one day, out of the blue during math, he blurted, "Do you have a family member or someone you know who is gay?"

I answered the question simply. "I do not—or not that I am aware of at the moment."

"Then what's the deal with you sticking up for gay people all the time?" This student, may I add, was extremely bright but at the time was also extremely emotionally troubled.

"I stick up for everyone," I said. "Language is important. Words like that are not acceptable and will never be tolerated in our classroom community. Only language that supports and lifts up one another will be allowed. Your job now is to start thinking of words that do just that," I let him know, in front of everyone.

I remember giving homework to this one student that entailed coming up with ten vocabulary words that would be supportive, positive, and uplifting for all students in the classroom. I wanted him to begin carefully considering his word choices and write about what he knew regarding people who were lesbian/gay/bisexual/transgender and, most importantly, how this made him *feel*. Through that assignment, I discovered that this student was wrestling with his own sexuality, which I learned later resulted partly from experiencing sexual abuse at a young age. This was really important for me to learn about this student, and it changed our relationship for the better. Looking at the big picture with this particular individual made all the difference for the both of us.

      Life is full of words being said around us all the time—some kind, some derogatory, some clever, and some ignorant. Teachers can play a key role in showing their students how important language is and how a word they say can render them powerless—not powerful. Part of teaching children is to reaffirm the choice they have to exercise and expand their vocabulary in ways that are uplifting and helping society. It is also a teacher's job to model kindness and respect for others. It is our job to be tolerant, accept our students, feel empathy and teach students to do the same.

15
Health Wellness: Preventing the Cycle of Abuse

Part of teaching tolerance and acceptance includes teaching the importance of body awareness. This topic is so important but can be uncomfortable and difficult for some teachers. I have seen many students advance through elementary grades with little sense of establishing appropriate boundaries, respecting others' bodies, and, most importantly, keeping their bodies safe. I have witnessed kids inappropriately touching others in the hallways as well as kids trying to touch teachers inappropriately. I have also heard complaints from students, such as So-and-So was acting inappropriately on the playground. But because of the rushed school day and other constraints, teachers often feel ill equipped and unable to deal with such serious allegations and incidents. Consequently, many of these improper acts of touching are either overlooked or downplayed.

  Children are curious, and sexual behavior demonstrated at school can be part of that curiosity—or something more serious. Therefore, it is extremely important that we teach students how to define healthy and "safe" touch, how to distinguish between good and bad touch, and who should be doing the touching. Healthy body awareness needs to be part of the social and emotional learning taking place in schools. Helping students respect their bodies and others' will support sexual abuse prevention for years to come, in fact, I advocate that students receive this education much earlier than most public schools allow.

There are great resources, programs, and services available that help public and private schools around the country educate students on how to respect their bodies. Learning to respect one's body is not something that comes naturally to children and must be taught. These services can also assist students who may have been or are being affected by physical or sexual abuse. They even include opportunities and presentations for children in preschool and the early elementary grades. Parents always have the option to opt out of having their child be a part of such programming, although this is unfortunate. The health curriculum often does not allow children much younger than fifth grade to discuss sexual anatomy and body awareness in any detail, but it needs to happen much earlier and more consistently.

If you have developed a strong human connection with your students and work hard to earn their respect and trust, chances are that you will be approached by one student—or more than one—with a report of abuse during your teaching career. Approximately one in six boys and one in four girls is sexually abused before the age of eighteen (The National Child Traumatic Stress Network, "Child Sexual Abuse Fact Sheet, (http://nctsn.org/nctsn_assets/pdfs/caring/ChildSexualAbuseFactSheet.pdf). So, statistically speaking, there will be students within your classrooms who are in fact experiencing this terrible reality. And if your teaching career is somewhat lengthy, you will also probably *suspect* that certain students may be experiencing physical or sexual abuse. Therefore, it is essential that teachers are trained to recognize the signs of abuse and how to best respond.

By law, teachers are required to report a suspected or known incidence of child abuse or neglect to child protective services. Please do this. I know it can be scary and overwhelming, and you might fear how it will affect the student, or if it will even do any good. But it is the right thing to do, not just legally, but for the child. Learning that one of my female students was being sexually abused was one of the most difficult and defining moments for me as a teacher.

It was my fourth year teaching a fourth-fifth split-grade class. The class was super challenging behaviorally, with extreme ranges in academic needs. I was at a progressive elementary school and it was the first time I had been presented with the opportunity to have a wonderful local organization specializing in sexual abuse prevention come to my classroom to present. All of my students had received permission to hear the two-part presentation and I was excited for them and for myself. The presentation was impressive, intense, interactive, very age appropriate, and spot-on for my students; I could tell we all had mixed reactions. The presentation ended with an opportunity for students to ask questions or speak privately to a presenter with a concern or question. Most kids left and went to lunch, but some stayed behind to ask questions.

Unbeknownst to me, one of my female students spoke with a presenter in the hallway. While I was eating lunch in my room, the presenter approached me without my student present and said she needed to share some information with me and was asked to by my student. Apparently, my student was uncomfortable with the way her father had been kissing her good night. She also provided some other details to the presenter that were disturbing and raised red flags. After school that day, I asked to talk to this student one-on-one. I let her know that I knew what had been shared earlier that day and what process needed to occur as a result. Above all, I wanted to make sure she was all right and determine whether there was anything else I could do to help.

  I filed my report that afternoon with child protective services and let my administrator know that I had done so. To my surprise, the follow-up with the child welfare agent was swift. I had filed reports on students for other suspicions before, and usually the child welfare professional (on the other end of the toll-free number) and follow-up on their end was slow to nonexistent, depending on the "severity" (their words, not mine) of the issue. So I was shocked that within a week of my confidential report, there had been a call placed and a visit made to this student's home. My administrator at the time was already aware of the situation from the presenter who had talked to my student, and she was concerned that this incident could stir up trouble for me and for my student and, I quote, it could "get ugly." She also said she hoped I knew what I was doing. I found her remark odd, but it also troubled me—it seemed to reflect a lack of support, like I was making more work or making things more difficult.

Sometimes it takes bravery as a teacher to follow our intuition and trust what will be best for our students, even when there is a lack of support in doing so, as was the case here.

Soon after making my report, a child welfare advocate interviewed my student in private at school. When the interview was finished, the child welfare professional asked to speak with me after school. She mentioned that things were getting worse. I sat down face-to-face with my student and had her tell me exactly what was happening at home and what she shared in the interview. The whole time I never once doubted what she was telling me. She was nervous and gave me uncomfortable details of interactions that had been going on for a while at night once her mom was asleep. She also mentioned her father smelling of alcohol and often drinking too much. She was specific about how what he was doing did not "feel okay" to her and made her very uncomfortable.

    A week after the interview, child protective services called the home and requested a home visit, explaining to the parents for the first time what had happened and what their daughter had revealed. The parents were outraged, as expected, and called the school immediately to request a meeting with my administrator. Caseworkers are typically not allowed to reveal who reported the information, so the parents were not aware it was me. That is, until my administrator told them, and I was encouraged (it felt more like being coaxed) to be a part of the meeting too.

    The parents were high profile and had offered much resource support to the school. I was not sure if my administrator's willingness to reveal my identity was to repair some relationship with the parents or to pacify their anger. I let my admin know that this was crushing the spirit of confidentiality, and my student's confidence as well. I let her know I would participate but would not be doing any talking. Big mistake. Attending that meeting was a mistake. The meeting was awful. The father let us know how outrageous the allegations were and how they had caused serious turmoil for their family. The wife looked terribly sad and appeared like she had not slept for some time. It was uncomfortable and not productive. It made me feel extreme sadness for my precious student and the need to defend her against these two people. Two months later, the case was determined "unsubstantiated," with a lack of evidence to prove suspected sexual abuse, and was dropped by child protective services. I went through the rest of that school year feeling like I had let down my student and failed in the end. Our relationship was never quite the same, and she often felt distant and cold during our interactions. There was mention that her parents had recently separated, and I wondered if things had changed for her at home. Did she regret ever coming forward in the first place?

    It was the last day of the school year and filled with the usual excitement of students. Gifts for me were deposited on my desk. I said good-bye to each student and felt the bittersweet feelings teachers can relate to in letting go of students we closely guided and taught for the preceding nine and a half months. Soon after the departure of students, I sadly began sifting through cards and sweet tokens of appreciation. There was a card at the very bottom from this very student that meant everything to me. I still have this card today. The greeting on the front read:

> There are many people who come and go in our lives. A few touch us in ways that change our lives forever, making us better from knowing them. You have made a difference in my life, and for this I am grateful.

And below was the student's signature and a note:

> Thanks so much for standing behind me 100% all the way. I appreciate the way you have been helping me. Know that it'll be okay. You have helped make it okay. Thanks so much!! . . . Thanks for being you . . and helping me be me.

What I learned from that whole experience with my female student was invaluable:

- Believe your students. Stand behind them one hundred percent. Make sure they know you have their backs—always! Even if for some reason the student has fabricated a story, there is a reason why, and still something may not be right. Chances are, most are telling you the truth ninety-nine percent of the time.

- Stand your ground and do what you feel is right. Things have changed since I was in that classroom, and hopefully the protocol for handling child abuse matters has as well. My administrator should have never affirmed my identity as the referral source and should have left it ambiguous as to who the caller may have been. My student never told them who had made the report, and they would not have conclusively known it was me, though they could have guessed. It was unprofessional and ineffective for me to be part of the meeting between the parents and the administrator. Plus, it was not beneficial to the most important person in this situation, my student!! Trust your gut instincts and stand your ground. Also, know your rights!!
- Do your best and be at peace with the results. Things may not turn out as expected, and sometimes life has limitations and events out of your control. Do not beat yourself up. Take care of yourself and applaud your efforts in trying your

best to do everything possible to love, protect, and provide the best outcome for your students. That is all you can do and it is okay.

- Students know you care, and when you have tried your best, they really do. This knowledge will last a lifetime in their memory of you as a teacher.
- Expect the unexpected. Difficult situations and experiences come with teaching, but they come with positive insights and lessons on how we can do better. Educating teachers and administrators on how best to report issues of suspected abuse and handle what comes next is in the best interest of the students and teachers. The same can be said for educating teachers and administrators on how to develop a more preventative health curriculum on body awareness and keep our students safe.
- Be clear and professional with regard to protocol when needing to file a report with social services on behalf of a student. Be clear on what guidelines to follow, but always keep in mind the best interest of the student first. Trust your instincts and let them guide your approach.

- Find support in school counselors and school social workers.

A friend and social worker helped me understand the signs of abuse and appropriate reactions to students displaying normal or abnormal sexual behavior at school. She also taught me that it is important that school staff not over- or underreact or respond to children's sexual behavior at school in a way that labels and "pathologizes" them.

It is the adult response to the child's behavior that gives the behavior meaning for the child. There needs to be a clear understanding and definition of what could be considered normal curiosity at a very young age versus inappropriate sexual behavior in upper elementary and older that would be harmful to oneself and others.

A year after the incident occurred and my student was in middle school, I was attending my local gym with my soon-to-be husband. I was stretching away from the workout area with headphones on and zoned out. I opened my eyes to find the father of that student standing above me. I was in shock initially. He said hello and asked how I was. I replied "well." He said he had heard I was getting married soon and asked how teaching was going. Again, I answered "yes" and "well." I decided I would not engage

147

any further and felt he may start trying to intimidate me. The last thing he said was the name of my former student and that she was doing really well. I nodded, simply walked away, and that was the end of that. I remember locking myself in the bathroom stall at the gym and just sitting for a while, shaking and confused. That was the last time I ever saw this person until just recently while attending a local TEDx. I pointed him out from a distance to my husband, who remembered the whole event and I quietly wished my student well.

    I think of all the individuals out there living with the reality of having been physically or sexually abused. We know who some are, but many people we know may be hiding this secret. Think of how many lives have been disrupted from abuse, as well as those who may even perpetuate the cycle of abuse. What if teachers could make a difference in helping students avoid this path by teaching skills and techniques to prevent the likelihood of abuse? That is really educating children to be happy, well, healthy, and productive individuals—uplifted individuals who go out into the world and take social action toward helping others.

Section V
Necessary Practice: Social and Emotional Learning

"A child who is protected from all controversial ideas is as vulnerable as a child who is protected from every germ. The infection, when it comes—and it will come—may overwhelm the system, be it the immune system or the belief system."

—Jane Smiley, Pulitzer Prize-winning American novelist.

16

Learning "Dangerous Truths" Through Literature

I realized the importance of teaching social-emotional learning to students early in my career. I was a new teacher in a fourth-grade classroom and working toward a master's degree simultaneously. I had a special opportunity to work with another fantastic first-year teacher and our graduate professor, who was a passionate and inspirational teacher for all preservice teachers who came in contact with her. This wonderful professor invited my colleague and I to co-author academic articles researching how teachers could help students think critically about serious issues by connecting more deeply to literature. The research focused on teacher read-alouds to students and the subsequent questions, comments, and actions that resulted from students interacting with the material.

Our professor suggested we use multicultural children's literature in our classrooms as a starting point in selecting books themed upon real life issues—stories showing racism, depression, abuse, tolerance, empathy, and sexual identity. Additionally, by using "authentic" literature, the books chosen often showed characters overcoming and finding resolution in the midst of these real life challenges. Our article was eventually published in the academic journal *Language Arts.*

At the time this article came out, the books chosen were considered heavily controversial by some educators, parents, school districts, religious groups, and others. The hypothesis was that through reading such books, students would show increased comprehension, more excitement to read, the ability to draw real life connections from the characters (who they would often identify with), and the books would stimulate meaningful discussion. Therefore, reading these books would improve academic success in reading and writing through social and emotional learning themes found in children's literature.

Doing this project in my classroom gave me confidence and conviction in using multicultural literature to teach important topics of racism, acceptance, sexual identity, and other "dangerous truths" that many teachers shy away from. I was also willing to take more risks by introducing books with the end goal of students asking hard questions, evolving into honest, nurturing discussions and helping students feel safe and part of a supportive community. This is not to say that fairytales aren't wonderful—they offer the ability to teach basic components of story and reading skills, such as making inferences and predicting outcomes—but fairy tales provide a happily ever after all the time, unlike real life.

Myself, my colleague and professor, who soon became my dear friends and mentors, went on to publish other articles that demonstrated the ability to teach social and emotional wellness to students through teaching "brave" texts and taking risks as teachers to incorporate literature that was not typically taught to young children.

My experience with reading books that held pages full of real and tough issues facing kids today showed how kids rise to high expectations and can handle difficult issues by learning to trust that they are capable and, in some cases, able to end cycles of abuse. It also deepened my teaching practice and added passion to my purpose of creating learning for students that connected to their real life experiences as seen through the eyes of the books' characters. Reading material that inspires kids to be brave and realize they are not alone in the challenges they face is more effective and meaningful than once upon a time.

Learning Opportunities through Literature: Drama, Art, Social Change

Reading books about characters that students can relate to offers learning opportunities that are useful and engaging. Useful and "real life" fictional texts provide students insights into the real world, allowing them to know it is okay to share difficult feelings, experiences, and desires and know they are not alone.

Some of the follow-up activities we did with students used drama and art to show what students were learning and in ways that were enjoyable for them. Here are some examples of how to use drama and art as powerful responses to literature:

- **Freeze frames.** Read a passage or a particular scene from a book and have one or more students capture the emotion through movement while others observe their different interpretations. (I found that groups of three work well.) You can also have a student read from the book. Then the reader loudly says "FREEZE," and the students strike a pose and hold it for the class to see. Students enjoy both dramatizing literature and watching their peers perform. Lots of fun for everyone!

- **Acting out.** Form small groups and have students put together skits interpreting what is happening within a particular passage. You can have students act out the same passage or provide different passages of their choosing. Then have them perform their skits in front of the whole class. Fascinating and fun!

- **Bring on the art! Paper cutouts, use of color.** This was one of my favorite activities. Students can create their own shapes or tear paper shapes that represent select characters. I also created colored geometric shapes and had students select characters that represented each shape based on color and shape design. It was fascinating to hear students explain why they selected the shape they did for a character and how color influenced this decision. It encouraged higher-level thinking and required students to develop oral presentation skills.

- **Character posters.** Students can make "Wanted" posters of characters in the book and provide detailed descriptions of a character's likes/dislikes, personality, physical characteristics (using imagination), and invent who would be the family, friends, or pets of this character . . . and more.

- **Mock letter to school board.** My colleague involved in the research project had her students write a mock letter to the school district explaining the value to students of reading controversial books. If you do this activity, discuss with students beforehand why a school district might consider censorship or require that certain grade-level standards be met before selecting such controversial material. I was amazed how my students, like myself, held such deep convictions about reading literature that went beyond "once upon a time."

Reading literature can also inspire students to become vehicles of social change in their school and extended communities. My students who shared common experiences with the characters in the books became involved in volunteering and setting up programs to help children and animals who were victims of abuse. They also wrote real letters to school boards and school district employees regarding the importance of reading books like the ones we read. Students found hope and comfort knowing they were not alone in their personal experience. They discovered that by being able to admit real challenges and problems that life throws our way, there is the possibility to come out the other door healthy and supported.

"Dangerous Truths" Open Minds

When my oldest daughter shared her seventh-grade reading list with me, I was surprised and thrilled by the selection. Her brave seventh-grade language arts teachers had included a very controversial book for the students to read. The book, *Sold,* by Patricia McCormick, is about a thirteen-year-old Nepalese girl sold into prostitution by her stepfather and mother. It is both shocking and grueling at times to read that horrific account of human trafficking, which is real and rampant in many parts of the world.

I wrote an e-mail to my daughter's teacher detailing my support and gratitude for such a book selection. She informed me that there had been a mistake and the book was actually district approved for ninth-grade, not seventh-grade, so students would not be reading the book as a class. However, students who had already purchased it would be able to read it individually at home with parental consent. This teacher later informed me that many parents had objected to this book selection, and she appreciated my ability to understand her vision behind having students read such a thought-provoking and well-written text.

My daughter ended up reading the book, and I allowed my ten-year-old daughter to read it as well. I trusted they could both handle the material and I was there to support questions and discussion. Parts of the book deeply troubled the three of us, and the difficult subject matter provided opportunities to discuss mature topics on sexual boundaries and body awareness. Both daughters were struck by the fact that they were the same ages as female characters in the book. The reality that many young girls across the world experience this trauma routinely throughout their lives was an eye opener. We also discussed the different roles men and women have in other cultures, what is considered acceptable work, and the hierarchy of power within parts of the world stricken with poverty and oppression. My younger daughter was inspired to write a letter to the author telling her how she felt about the book and what she learned. She asked me what we could do to help. I turned the question back on her: *What can we do to help?* We researched organizations working to abolish human trafficking and educate and remove young girls trapped in this web of destruction.

Both girls appreciate their circumstances and understand how different the world can be for other girls their ages. These "dangerous truths" they were exposed to in literature have opened their minds and allowed them to become more tolerant of differences, more empathetic, and more intolerant of worldly injustices.

* * *

We continue to feel children are only capable of handling so much and protect them from what they deserve to know. In limiting their exposure, we limit their ability for tolerance and social and emotional wellness. Through literary experiences, teachers can offer a safe place to hold discussions and explore serious issues of racism, abuse, drug addiction, depression, divorce, and topics of sexuality requiring understanding and compassion. By teaching from a place of respect and high expectations, children rise to the occasion.

Selecting brave and authentic multicultural literature as part of your reading library is part of a preventative approach to bullying and feelings of isolation—it connects students on issues and builds trust and empathy within the classroom. There are programs to "manage" bullying and recommended disciplinary actions once the act of bullying has occurred. But we must place more emphasis on preventing it in the first place.

It is hard to underestimate the impact of social and emotional skills on a child's schooling life and future career. Teaching social and emotional wellness through literature provides great opportunities for positive impact, social confidence, and can lead your students to taking social action.

17
Service Learning Breeds Spirit

Many schools have spirit weeks and spirit days where students support school values and mascots by wearing T-shirts and school colors. These endeavors, though well intentioned, are not in keeping with what is useful and beneficial for students, and they do not satisfy the goal of promoting wellness for teachers or students. In my years of teaching, I have not seen a spirit day, week, or assembly that inspires change, well-being, or social action. In one case, a week was dedicated to eradicating bullying and promoting school kindness and respect by having students and teachers dress up in different themed outfits. Actual e-mail and signs looked like this:

SPIRIT WEEK—NEXT WEEK: MAY 2nd–MAY 6th

- Monday: Pajama Day—Say Goodnight to Bullying

- Tuesday: Tropical Day—Wash Out Bullying

- Wednesday: Disney Day—Put Bullying in the Dungeon

- Thursday: Sports Day—Knock Bullying Out of the Park

- Friday: 50s Day—Send Bullying Cruising Down the Road

How as teachers can we support spirit weeks where the mission is dressing up in random clothing, which can be fun, but is not useful to what really needs to be addressed, namely helping to prevent the big outcome of bullying. Having students dress up in Disney wear or in 1950s clothing does not teach empathy, respect of cultural differences, anti-bullying skills, nor does it help students learn social and emotional skills that will aid in future schooling or in the workforce.

In my experience, this type of event creates more distraction from the learning day and a diversion from the greater issue at hand. I actually heard teachers say the idea of dressing up caused more disruption in the classroom from kids being concerned about getting costumes to wear, parents e-mailing and calling about why kids were dressing up, and what happens once students arrive in Disney outfits. Let's have higher expectations for students.

I am curious what the takeaway was for kids. Wearing pajamas wipes out bullying? I heard one female fourth-grader ask "Was there even bullying in the 50s?" trying to make meaning of the poster advertising the spirit week lineup. Schools have a habit of putting a Band-Aid on problems and hoping they will go away.

One highly effective strategy for inspiring change, wellness, and social action (and a superior alternative to spirit weeks) is service learning—and I am a big proponent. The benefits to implementing service learning, or "passion projects," as I like to call them, are many.

Benefits of Service Learning

Service learning projects help students develop useful real life skills: leadership, collaboration, communication, and accountability—beginning with a focus issue, creating a project, determining who will be helped through action, and following through till the end goal is met.

Determining social issues that students want to learn more about and take action on affords an opportunity to really get to the root cause of the issue at hand. Students then connect these causes to their own actions in or outside the classroom. This effort breeds the idea of how "our" actions affect those around us and makes it about the collective whole. One student may be passionate about dog rescues that are "no-kill shelters" and then find such a group in India that needs support in order to educate the community and obtain funding to stay operational. Another student might value sexual/reproductive health for young women in parts of Africa where education and medical supplies can be sparse, and thus find a solution or an organization to partner with in finding a solution.

Service learning allows students to shine in other ways that academic teaching does not always permit. Students who are usually not leaders in small- or large-group settings become more confident about sharing and organizing their "passion project" with others. Also, creative talents are allowed to be a major component in using art, music, and other skills to design presentations on students' chosen projects.

Public speaking is another big part of sharing service learning to classmates, parents, and other teachers. Helping kids develop public-speaking skills in school is invaluable. Finally, students will realize that they can make a difference, no matter who or how old they are. This builds confidence in knowing that they can achieve their dreams and help others achieve theirs as well.

Next time your school wants to hold a science fair or spelling bee, hold a service learning fair instead! It can help students understand and learn about diverse cultures and communities. This type of school project can be viewed in an auditorium and will inspire other students, parents, and community members. It can even be a large schoolwide project, with each grade level contributing as appropriate. Also, consider providing opportunities for students to collaborate virtually with other students and schools across the globe.

18
Indigenous Education

Among some educators in the United States, there is the belief that a Western model of education is the only way to provide a "better, more prosperous" life for non-indigenous and indigenous children alike. Recently, however, there has been a shift toward recognizing the benefits of indigenous education within the public school system. Because we are all indigenous to somewhere, it serves us to remember and gain insight into the significance of indigenous cultures and ancient spiritual traditions. Indigenous education focuses on social and emotional learning and allows for students to understand that they are part of something bigger than themselves.

Including indigenous knowledge and wisdom in the public school system can greatly enrich our students' learning experience. I would like to see more teachers, parents, and administrators advocate for integrating educational practices that are sensitive to and honor cultural differences and that draw upon practical and effective uses of indigenous approaches, thus taking public education beyond the Western-driven curriculum of math, reading, and writing.

Indigenous education focuses a student's learning through student observation, storytelling and narrative, and collaboration and cooperation among peers and adults. This hands-on approach emphasizes direct experience and learning through "inclusion." There are many definitions of inclusion in public education, but in the case of indigenous education, it means children feel they are vital members of the community and are encouraged to participate in a meaningful way by those members of the community—teachers, parents, elders, and leaders. Children effectively learn skills through this system, without being taught in a formal manner that is often teacher driven.

This differs from Western learning approaches, which typically have a central learning authority and tend to include methods such as explicit and specific instruction, testing (and more testing), and quizzing. Consider an educational environment for children that is mindful of cultural differences, rather than an education that follows a homogenized Western format. This could allow for a child to retain knowledge more easily, since they are learning in a way that was successful for ancestral communities. I believe all children can benefit from instruction that creates learning consistent to their culture and upbringing. This goes hand in hand with helping students to feel useful and supported in becoming a valued community member.

Feeling Important in Indigenous Education

As mentioned above, indigenous education emphasizes the importance of students feeling that they are a vital member of the community. I do not believe that Western education necessarily encourages children to feel important within their greater communities. There is a lot of competition and focus on the individual over group success. As teachers, we need to make children feel like valued members of their classroom community and create an awareness of how each child's success is furthered when working together with others. This feeling of importance can extend to how student actions can be taken for the betterment of society, where students feel confident and able to make change.

In our current advanced technological world, where devices do much of the communicating between youths and between adults, let us not lose sight of the value of the hands-on connection and what has served us well in the past. When teachers revisit learning that involves participation and strengthens relationships between the parent-teacher-student, this decreases students feeling isolated and questioning their greater purpose.

Contrasts: Western and Indigenous Education

There are many differences within the Western and indigenous models of education. I believe that indigenous education holds beneficial tools for educating all children. Indigenous education provides an inclusive approach that is centered around the school community, which supports and addresses the individual needs of each child.

Western classrooms define a clear distinction between classroom and community: Classrooms are modeled after the teacher taking an authoritative role while regurgitating information for students to learn and memorize for future skill-based assessments. The indigenous structure tends to remove the distinction between community and classroom, emphasizing cooperative learning and group learning based on what will be useful in indigenous societies and in professional work, and also what skills will benefit the community at large.

Teachers within the Western structure are not taught the importance of balancing personal warmth and empathy with the demand for academic success, much less how to do so. The role of human connection is generally not considered crucial for administrators either. Teachers who choose to adopt indigenous methods often view the teacher-student relationship as constructed in a way that the teacher shares the control of the classroom with the students. Teachers are co-learning with students and strive to maintain a balance between personal warmth and the demand for academic achievement. This balance lends itself to feeling happy and well within this dynamic relationship between teacher and students.

Indigenous classrooms encourage all students to participate in classroom discourse. Direct questions are posed to the group rather than the teacher, as is common in Western settings. Students are not singled out for praise, criticism, or recitation, though praise is used when students demonstrate effort given rather than answering question correctly. Additionally, students are allowed to move about freely within the classroom and are trusted to consult with other students. Knowing they are trusted enables them to stay on task and feel more vested in living up to these expectations and responsibilities.

Confusion with Inclusion

Inclusion as defined in Western education often refers to the placement of students with disabilities in general education classes. I worked as a paraprofessional for a period of time and followed the *Inclusion Model* as it relates to special education within the public school system.

Inclusion should not simply mean the placement of students with disabilities in general education classes. It must also incorporate fundamental changes in the way a school supports and addresses the individual needs of each child and the skills they will need in and out of the classroom. In Western education, students are given activities and assignments determined mostly by the teacher. There is not always a choice of topic or lesson, and there is a lack of student-directed learning based on the student's goals and interests.

Indigenous inclusion within education means children should be involved in a range of activities in which they actively contribute to community endeavors. Activities that are often viewed as "chores" within Western schooling are instead viewed as necessities in helping the classroom, one's family, and the greater community.

Students actively participate in their learning, and they are given choices to select activities that are useful and interesting to them. These learning activities are within the context of what students may want to pursue in their future schooling or career.

Learning Pace

In indigenous education, children learn based on their individual motivation. Independence is given to children to develop skills at their own pace and when they are ready. I believe this approach is crucial in helping students to be successful academically and socially within the school environment. I value how the indigenous approach honors maturity and the ability for children to handle social and academic rigor before they are pushed into a grade level or activity they are perhaps not yet ready to handle. In the Western model, children are expected to master a skill or demonstrate knowledge in a content area by a certain time and age, which often interferes with where the child is developmentally. The Western pace is rigorous at times, and certainly not enough time is allotted for in-depth, hands-on learning and activities.

During the latter part of my public school career, I

worked with students who were early accessed into kindergarten or first grade by the request of a parent. The school district allowed for this placement after students took a series of tests. The tests were administered at the school district headquarters by a team of adults who worked in advanced academic services and who the children had more than likely never met before. I was told that these tests measured "advanced academic performance," but as a talented and gifted coordinator, I was not privy to the tests used or told how exactly the advanced placement was determined. I asked one teacher of a student granted early access about what information had been given to her. "Nothing," was her response. The teacher had requested information, but it was never provided. This lack of communication does not seem supportive of teachers or students by the powers that be.

    What I do know is what I observed. My feeling is that it was usually difficult, even detrimental, for students, especially boys, to be granted this early access. I have only known two accelerated female students who appeared to benefit from such action, but only two. Let me be very clear: I am not saying that acceleration in subject areas is not beneficial for students—this action can be appropriate and valuable. What I am suggesting is that in the early ages of elementary school, it may be too early to identify academic or creative "giftedness" in students. Moreover, students who appear to be doing above average by academic standards may be lacking in social and emotional wellness and maturity.

    I followed one student early accessed into kindergarten (barely age four) through second grade and worked with him during my stint as a talented and gifted coordinator. Each school year he experienced more behavioral issues and struggled to "fit in" with peers and "maintain friendships." His mother expressed these words to me one day while helping out in the classroom, and she did not understand why her son was socially "awkward." This parent then decided to follow the same pattern with early access for this student's younger female sibling. I really wanted to ask this parent what the end game was for her children. Harvard at age sixteen? Youngest person to work for NASA? This student lacked support from his classroom environment to provide the adequate social and emotional wellness needed for his overall well-being—and to help him succeed with future schooling and a career. I had many students like him who needed this support, so while working with this young group, I made this my main focus.

I understand parents opting for what they believe to be better for their children, but sometimes they may "push" their children too fast or in the wrong direction. As human connection "guru" Rita Pierson stated during one of her TED talks: "Parents make decisions for their children based on what they know, what they feel will make them safe and well. And it is not our place [as educators] to say what they do is 'wrong.' It's our place to say maybe we can add a set of rules that they don't know about." It is a teacher's place to set forth guiding structures, fair for kids, which leave students feeling empowered as a result—rules that allow for success and setting students up for growth.

Motivation and Assessment

In the Western educational system, motivation is typically measured by grades and assessments. Students are labeled motivated or unmotivated, or "lazy student" or "good student" (as I have heard voiced by teachers). In Western classrooms, teachers are held as the central learning authority and are responsible for motivating students. This role is not the most beneficial or empowering for teachers.

174

Motivation is often viewed on the theory that there is one single way to learn, and students feel pressured to fit into this narrow expectation, leading to an unsuccessful learning environment.

In indigenous cultures, there is appreciation for the extended community and ancient spiritual traditions. Teachers are trusted and respected in indigenous cultures and demonstrate the freedom to facilitate learning success. Teachers following indigenous approaches provide freedom for their students to direct their personal motivation levels into what they will learn, which creates autonomy and choice in areas of study.

Indigenous approaches also encourage student assessments and evaluations. Western classrooms value student self-assessments, but the final determination of grades and the final evaluation is always by the teacher. Assessments and evaluations in indigenous education involve the teacher, parents, and community members. Assessments are for the purpose of supporting students, and they come from a place of acceptance of where the students are in their learning; corrections are given if it helps increase understanding. Assessments assist students as they actively participate in an activity. Adequate time is allotted for students to master a task, plus there is constant feedback on their learning progress and self-evaluations as well.

The indigenous model of evaluating students on an ongoing basis and discussing the evaluations with them is very different from traditional Western report cards that are subjective and issued only two to three times a year. Conferences offer feedback, but these scheduled conferences are brief and the student often is not present. I am a fan of student-led conferences that put students in charge of explaining their learning (so they understand) and showcase examples of their work and areas of improvement. Also, I prefer student portfolios instead of report cards. I know firsthand it is more work for teachers, but having students show work samples and select pieces of evidence demonstrating student growth and learning is invaluable.

Schools say that standardized tests are one form of assessment that helps inform teachers and administrators as to what is being taught and how to teach better. I disagree. Standardized tests are scored and reviewed by an unknown entity, with no relationship to actual teachers, students taking the tests, or school administrators. There is no sense of inclusion or community, and students are unable to see their own test to improve upon mistakes. Plus, the material on state tests does not present opportunities to demonstrate a process in solving a problem or mastering a task.

The Cycle of Control

"One of the most profound changes that occurs when modern schooling is introduced into traditional societies around the world is the radical shift from the locus of power and control over learning from children, families, and communities to ever more centralized systems of authority," writes Carol Black in her blog post "Occupy Your Brain: On Power, Knowledge, and Re-occupation of Common Sense (http://schoolingtheworld.org/blog/occupy/). Black directed and edited a film called *Schooling the World*, the same name as her fantastic blog. Black explains that in societies that are considered not modernized, children learn through many mediums like free play, lots of interaction with multiple children and adults, absorption in nature, directly helping adults with work, and communal activities. Black also emphasizes that children "learn by experience, experimentation, trial and error, by independent observation of nature and human behavior, and through a voluntary community sharing of information, story, song and ritual."

In indigenous education, adults have little control over students' moment-to-moment movements and choices, she writes, adding that once learning becomes "institutionalized," the freedom of the individual and their respect for elder or ancient wisdom dissolves. In the traditional Western educational system, "family and community are sidelined. . . . The teacher has control over the child, the school district has control over the teacher, the state has control over the district, and increasingly, systems of national standards and funding creates national control over states," Black writes.

I suggest the Western educational system consider the following:

- Shift control to connection, collaboration, and cooperation between the federal government, states, school districts, and other teachers.
- Allow teachers to create systems that empower and support other teachers, leading to healthy and happy students being taught by healthy and happy teachers.

- Respect differences and celebrate each individual as they are different in race, cultural and religious beliefs, and sexual and gender identity.

* * *

I believe teachers would benefit from exploring the possibility of how to incorporate indigenous aspects within their school classrooms. Creating a sense of community increases feelings of happiness and acceptance within the classroom, the school environment, and the extended community. The cohesive and respectful model of indigenous education focuses on the whole child, with an emphasis on belonging and serving something greater than oneself. I believe that incorporating an indigenous education model could discourage school violence by teaching students to respect differences within their school environment, giving students more autonomy and choice in their learning, and by promoting cultural awareness. This model reflects useful and empowering strategies that uplift students, teachers, and families in education that is fundamentally good.

19
Finland Has It Figured Out!

Finland takes care of its teachers. Teachers are happy in Finland. Finland highly respects its teachers and is a land where training educators is as important as training doctors. Teachers in Finland spend less hours at school each day and less time in classrooms compared to teachers in the United States.

Teachers build human connection with each other and their students and feel valued within their society. They are considered autonomous and given freedom and time to develop curriculum and assessments for students. Teachers in Finland are trusted that they will get the job done and done well and will meet the high expectations of the country's standards. Oh, did I not mention there are no mandated standardized tests in Finland?? Actually, there is one. The exam at the end of students' senior year of high school, which hardly counts.

Finland is also very mindful regarding personal time for students and teachers. I have read different "rules" and practices followed by Finnish educators, and one is that students need time for free time. There is a belief in

Finnish schools that kids will be most successful if they have a chance to refocus and ground their energy. It actually is a legal right of students to have fifteen minutes of free time every forty-five minutes of the school day. This, in theory, allows students to work more productively within the classroom when this time is balanced with the natural need to talk to others, play, move around, and even read quietly. Also, there is a belief that going outside encourages greater health and fitness.

Teachers benefit from the belief of valuing personal time for students. They have more relaxed and focused students, and productivity with learning is increased. They also have time to refocus and more energy dedicated to teaching because of these breaks. Everyone has the ability to become happier and well as a result.

Pasi Sahlberg, a Finnish education expert and the director of the Center for International Mobility and Cooperation in Finland's Ministry of Education and Culture, identifies the biggest obstacle in the U.S. educational system as being the same policy intended to revolutionize education. "If I could change one thing in policy, I would seriously rethink the role of standardized testing," he said in a 2012 interview with the *Stanford*

News. "No high-performing nation in the world has been successful using the policies that the United States is using," Sahlberg said, adding that he doesn't think standardized testing is inherently bad, but "the way it's done here is simply leading to so many negative consequences, in the form of narrowing curricula and reshaping the way teachers and schools are working,"(Stephen Tung, "How the Finnish School System Outshines U.S. Education," http://news.stanford.edu/news/2012/january/finnish-schools-reform-012012.html).

One more thing, Finland's students are a product of happy teachers. Unlike schools in the United States, Finland has decided to forgo using nationwide tests to evaluate schools, teachers, or students. Teachers are treated with trust and respect. Finland has high expectations for their teachers, so naturally they rise to the occasion like students do when they are trusted, given autonomy, and expected to rise to the occasion. I find this interesting—the parallels between the treatment and support of teachers in Finland and the treatment of students, and how both teachers and students are more successful as a result.

Here are some interesting facts to consider about teachers in Finland:

- The Finnish curriculum is focused on critical thinking, problem solving, project-based learning, and learning to learn. There is a great deal of collaboration in classrooms.
- Teachers in Finland are compared to, and held in as high regard as, lawyers, doctors, and architects.
- Teachers in Finland are required to obtain a three-year master's degree (state funded) before teaching. Many education positions are highly coveted. It is harder to get into a primary school education program (equivalent to an elementary certification program at a U.S. university) than a medical program in Finland (Tung).

Conclusion

"The purpose of education is to build a happier society; we need a more holistic approach that promotes the practice of love and compassion."
—The 14th Dalai Lama, February 20, 2017, Twitter.

Social and emotional wellness education, or affective education, needs to be as important as teaching math, reading, and writing on a daily basis. Teachers need to be proactive in seeking out curriculum and programming that promotes social skills, builds self-esteem and empathy, and promotes healthy body awareness. By reducing our need to label children and get to know them as individuals first, we can improve academic performance.

Social and emotional wellness can be part of any literacy program and can improve reading and writing skills, as well as develop oral and communication skills. Assessing student learning of books through art and dramatic expression allows students who might otherwise struggle with traditional literacy practices to be successful.

It is proven that increased social and emotional wellness not only increases academic success, it reduces school violence. It creates a culture of acceptance regardless of sexual orientation, race, socioeconomic status, or political differences.

More than ever, society is seeking positive citizens who are models of respect and kindness for today's students. Service learning prepares students to engage in social action beyond classroom walls, allowing positive global change to occur for humanity.

I do believe that feeling well and happy within the teaching profession is the recipe for happy and well students. Social and emotional learning is crucial in preparing students to be competent and content twenty-first-century individuals. Our goal as educators is to work together with students, parents, and community members to create uplifting institutions that support and stimulate innovative teaching and sustain creative energy for professional longevity.

If you are currently employed or entering into a profession working with children and gung ho to make a difference, remember to take care of yourself FIRST. Start a wellness revolution for yourself and for your colleagues. Let the change you make be contagious throughout your school and community beyond. Teachers will be and are the answer to changing education systems that are broken—starting one person at a time, one student at a time. Eventually, educators will be affecting school climates and structures, transforming public schools into quality institutions. The human connection created will foster professional success for teachers and academic success for students.

All it takes is someone like you to care a whole lot. Be happy. Teach well.

Acknowledgments

THANK YOU . . . !!!

John—my husband, my love, number one supporter, believer, and best friend.

Sydney and Ava, you both motivate and inspire me to spread more good in the world.

My parents and former educators, Tom and Karen. I love you both so much!

My sisters, Shelby and Hanley, for always cheering me on in all endeavors.

Kay and Jim Bird. Evelyn and Myron Hill. Your support is always felt.

Thomas Morgan – your social media savvy and guidance has been much appreciated!

Jody Berman, editor extraordinaire and writing guru. Thank you for your support and guidance throughout this process. I so appreciate and value working with you! You helped my dream come true.

Some of the best, most hardworking and supportive teachers, administrators, professors and social workers who encouraged and inspired me during my career to now: Darcy Ballentine, Amy Kahn Scheff, Penny Scott-Oliver, Jeff Oliver, Dana Vallely Covington, Nimia Nelson, Khara West, and Julie Tarnowski-Marks.

CPSIA information can be obtained
at www.ICGtesting.com
Printed in the USA
BVHW031924051218
534867BV00001B/44/P